6th Grad
All Subject
Workbook

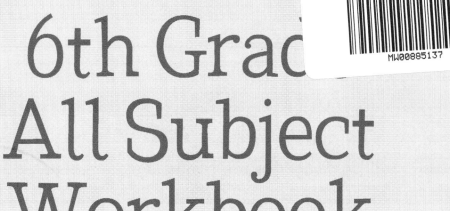

Thank you for choosing Clever Home Curriculum.

We value your honest feedback. If you find this workbook useful, please be sure to rate it on Amazon!

"Wisdom begins in wonder."

Socrates

THIS WORKBOOK BELONGS TO:

TRANSLATING ALGEBRAIC EXPRESSIONS

Rewrite each word problem as an algebraic statement

1) 9 less than 4 times z

_____

2) 8 is subtracted from n

_____

3) 6 minus h

_____

4) 4 times the sum of 9 and k

_____

5) k minus 2

_____

6) 8 times the sum of p and 5

_____

7) Two-fifths of the sum of w and 7 minus the product of 6 and g

_____

8) Subtract two-thirds from 8 times q

_____

9) Four-fifths of the sum of w and 9 plus the product of 8 and x

_____

10) Sum of d and 3

_____

TRANSLATING ALGEBRAIC EXPRESSIONS

Rewrite each word problem as an algebraic statement

1) Add one-fourth to 9 times x   _____

2) Subtract three-fourths from 6 times k   _____

3) z squared plus the product of 9 and d plus 8   _____

4) s is added to 2   _____

5) Three-fifths of the sum of n and 6   _____

6) Take away 3 from 9 times c   _____

7) 4 is added to h   _____

8) 9 less than h   _____

9) Take away 7 from r   _____

10) 7 divided by n   _____

GEOGRAPHY & MAPS MATCH GAME

Match each term to the correct definition

longitude	latitude	equator	prime meridian
relative location	absolute location	isthmus	delta
mouth of river		monsoon	El Niño
La Niña	plateau		

1) the exact spot on Earth where a place is found

2) a measure of distance north or south of the equator

3) a narrow strip of land that joins two larger areas of land

4) a raised area of relatively level land

5) imaginary circle around Earth that divides it into northern & southern hemispheres

6) 0 degrees longitude from which other longitudes are calculated

7) a seasonal wind that brings great amounts of rain

8) part of the river that empties into another body of water

9) a weather pattern associated with drought in the southwestern United States

10) a triangular deposit of soil at the mouth of a river

11) a weather pattern associated with increased rainfall in South & Central America & in the USA

12) the location of one place in relation to other places

13) a measure of distance east or west of the prime meridian

GEOGRAPHY & MAPS MATCH GAME

Match each term to the correct definition

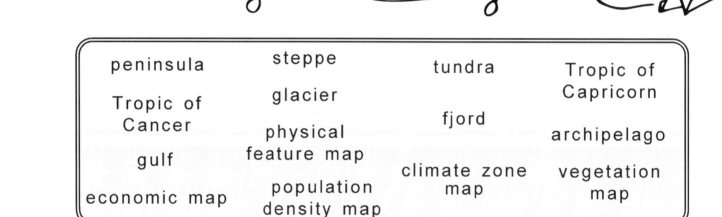

peninsula

steppe

tundra

Tropic of Capricorn

Tropic of Cancer

glacier

fjord

gulf

physical feature map

archipelago

climate zone map

vegetation map

economic map

population density map

1) shows the location of land forms such as deserts, mountains & plains

2) shows the trade, commerce, transport of goods & economic conditions of a region

3) shows the typical weather of a region

4) an extensive, usually treeless plain; often dry & grass-covered

5) southern line of latitude near the equator

6) a group of islands

7) cold, treeless plain with permanently frozen subsoil

8) northern line of latitude near the equator

9) a thick sheet of ice that moves slowly across land

10) long, narrow, deep inlet of the sea located between steep cliffs

11) shows the population of a region compared to total land area

12) depicts all the trees & plant life of a place, taken as a whole

13) a body of land surrounded by water on three sides

14) large inlet of an ocean, similar to a bay but often longer & more enclosed by land

SUPERSTAR SPELLING QUIZ

Identify the correct spelling of each word

1) A. inquiory   B. inquirey   C. inquiry   D. inquiery

2) A. flexibilitey   B. flexability   C. flexibility   D. flexibilaty

3) A. hilights   B. hilites   C. highlites   D. highlights

4) A. anticipaite   B. anticepate   C. anticipate   D. anticapate

5) A. renewabble   B. renewible   C. ranewable   D. renewable

6) A. interferense   B. innerference   C. interferance   D. interference

7) A. communitty   B. comunity   C. communitey   D. community

8) A. percaushion   B. precaution   C. percaution   D. precaushion

9) A. beuatifully   B. beautifuly   C. beautifully   D. beautifulley

10) A. ascending   B. assending   C. acsending   D. acending

11) A. rezounding   B. risounding   C. resounding   D. rasounding

12) A. maneuvers   B. manouvres   C. manuevers   D. manouvers

13) A. indiscribable   B. indiscribeable   C. indescribeable   D. indescribable

14) A. facillitate   B. facillatate   C. faccilitate   D. facilitate

15) A. triversed   B. traversed   C. traveresed   D. traverssed

SUPERSTAR SPELLING QUIZ

Identify the correct spelling of each word

1) A. reccollect   B. recolect   C. reccolect   D. recollect

2) A. sougt   B. soughtt   C. sought   D. souhgt

3) A. scrimmidge   B. scrimmige   C. scrimmege   D. scrimmage

4) A. colegiate   B. collegiate   C. collegate   D. colleigate

5) A. forreigner   B. foreigner   C. foriegner   D. foreignor

6) A. comittee   B. commitee   C. committee   D. committie

7) A. akword   B. awkward   C. awkword   D. akward

8) A. unconnvinced   B. unconvinced   C. unconvinct   D. unconvinsed

9) A. announsements   B. announcements   C. announcments   D. announcemints

10) A. extrordinarey   B. extraordinary   C. extraordanary   D. extrordinary

11) A. numerical   B. numericle   C. numerrical   D. numeracal

12) A. technolegy   B. tecknology   C. technolagy   D. technology

13) A. exhaussted   B. exhausted   C. eckshausted   D. exausted

14) A. newsworthy   B. newsworthey   C. newsworthie   D. newswerthy

15) A. miosture   B. moistcher   C. moisture   D. moissture

SURFACE AREA & VOLUME WITH SPHERES

Use 3.1416 for pi. Round answers to the nearest hundredth if needed

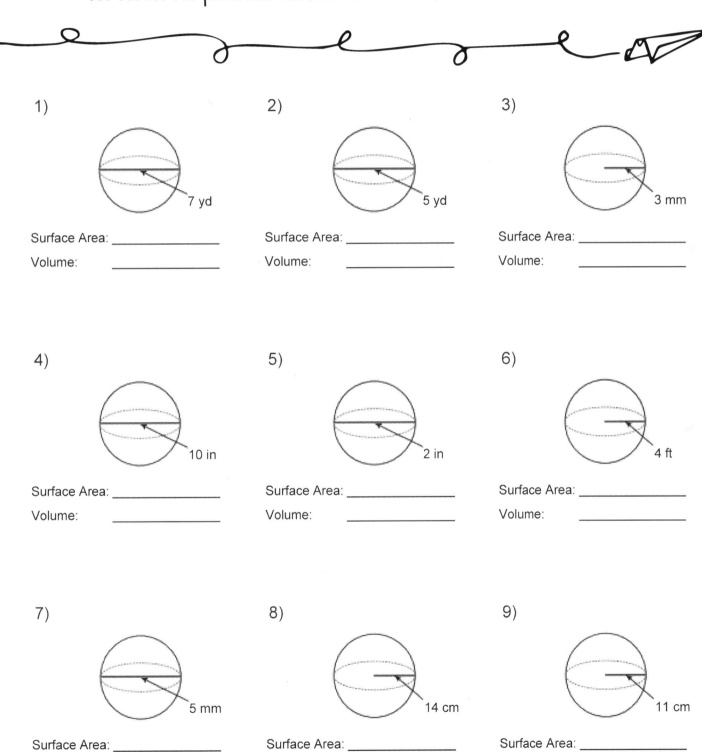

1)

7 yd

Surface Area: _____

Volume: _____

2)

5 yd

Surface Area: _____

Volume: _____

3)

3 mm

Surface Area: _____

Volume: _____

4)

10 in

Surface Area: _____

Volume: _____

5)

2 in

Surface Area: _____

Volume: _____

6)

4 ft

Surface Area: _____

Volume: _____

7)

5 mm

Surface Area: _____

Volume: _____

8)

14 cm

Surface Area: _____

Volume: _____

9)

11 cm

Surface Area: _____

Volume: _____

SURFACE AREA & VOLUME WITH SPHERES

Use 3.1416 for pi. Round answers to the nearest hundredth if needed

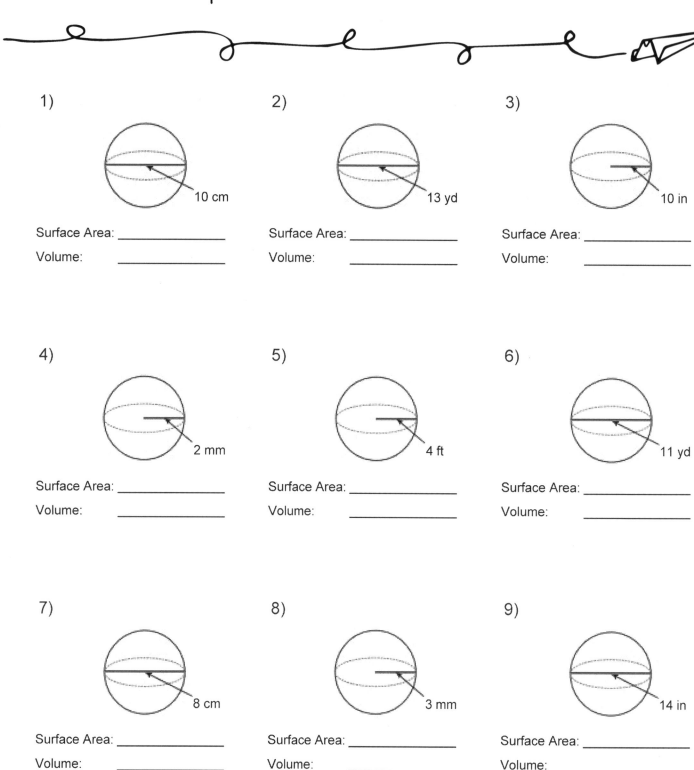

1)

10 cm

Surface Area: _____
Volume: _____

2)

13 yd

Surface Area: _____
Volume: _____

3)

10 in

Surface Area: _____
Volume: _____

4)

2 mm

Surface Area: _____
Volume: _____

5)

4 ft

Surface Area: _____
Volume: _____

6)

11 yd

Surface Area: _____
Volume: _____

7)

8 cm

Surface Area: _____
Volume: _____

8)

3 mm

Surface Area: _____
Volume: _____

9)

14 in

Surface Area: _____
Volume: _____

EARLY HUMANS WORD SEARCH

Find all the history terms in the word search below

adaptation	anthropologist	archaeologist	domestication
hunter gatherer	Neolithic	Paleolithic	paleontologist
hominids	agriculture	bipedal	Homo habilis
Homo erectus	Homo sapiens	Australopithecus	Neanderthal
primate	Stone Age	Mesolithic	prehistoric

```
P  D  G  H  O  M  O  H  A  B  I  L  I  S  S  H  V  I  K  O
D  G  F  A  V  K  D  A  W  H  U  E  R  Q  P  L  Y  H  J  Z
A  J  A  H  G  B  V  O  P  Q  H  N  D  E  G  F  K  O  X  Z
Z  V  L  U  U  R  M  D  M  H  O  M  I  N  I  D  S  M  B  H
M  Y  U  P  S  N  I  P  N  E  Z  R  P  F  L  C  J  O  I  A
I  E  K  A  A  T  T  C  A  E  S  W  D  F  L  T  Y  E  J  D
O  B  Y  L  K  N  R  E  U  L  O  T  H  L  E  F  U  R  Z  A
N  I  D  E  M  A  T  A  R  L  E  L  I  B  O  J  A  E  E  P
D  P  I  O  L  R  P  H  L  G  T  O  I  C  J  C  M  C  G  T
I  E  P  N  A  C  S  R  R  O  A  U  L  T  A  Y  F  T  C  A
B  D  R  T  N  H  K  T  I  O  P  T  R  I  H  T  T  U  W  T
O  A  E  O  A  A  G  R  O  M  P  I  H  E  T  I  I  S  P  I
Q  L  H  L  E  E  M  V  I  N  A  O  T  E  L  H  C  O  U  O
J  M  I  O  B  O  Q  X  E  U  E  T  L  H  R  O  I  N  N  N
S  K  S  G  P  L  U  O  G  R  M  A  E  O  E  E  Q  C  N  L
T  N  T  I  X  O  G  O  K  R  W  V  G  B  G  C  R  J  M  S
S  W  O  S  U  G  E  M  F  V  O  L  I  E  D  I  U  G  Q  H
M  Z  R  T  V  I  M  E  S  O  L  I  T  H  I  C  S  S  R  I
L  J  I  H  T  S  N  E  A  N  D  E  R  T  H  A  L  T  I  A
U  W  C  N  G  T  Y  A  L  H  O  M  O  S  A  P  I  E  N  S
```

FILL IN THE BLANKS: VOCABULARY

Decide which word best completes each sentence

abandon	arrogant	coherent	cosmetic
gavel	lenient	pending	tolerance
polarize	immense		

1) Despite his kind persona, the movie star was incredibly _____ in real life, believing himself to be better than other people because of his wealth and status.

2) An excited David hit the dance floor immediately, proceeding to do the robot with total _____.

3) The defendant's reply caused an uproar in the courtroom, requiring the judge to bang his _____ and demand "ORDER!" for a solid minute.

4) Jason knew his controversial opinion that pineapple should be mandatory on all pizzas would _____ the class.

5) As it turned out, Kate's school was pretty _____ about enforcing the dress code, and she made it through the entire day without being asked to remove her clown wig.

6) Thankfully, the damage to my car was purely _____ and didn't affect its functionality.

7) My grandpa eats ghost peppers every day, so his _____ for spicy foods is off the charts!

8) I figured Jacob must still be half-asleep, since his strange ramblings weren't the least bit _____.

9) With the order status stuck on _____, Beto couldn't be certain that his pre-order was actually secured.

10) The mansion was an _____ beast, featuring several helicopter pads and a designated room just for eating cake.

EXPLORING WORLD HISTORY

Choose the right answer for each question. Conduct research online as needed

1) Why did Stone Age people practice slash-and-burn agriculture?

   A. to drive away wild animals

   B. to make irrigation easier

   C. to fulfill spiritual beliefs

   D. to clear land for farming

2) Which development most enabled early people to form permanent settlements?

   A. advances in agriculture production

   B. advances in written language

   C. the creation of democratic government

   D. the spread of monotheism

3) Hammurabi's Code of ancient Mesopotamia was important because it:

   A. listed the laws and punishments

   B. established a single type of currency

   C. explained how the government officials were chosen

   D. described formal religious ceremonies

4) The art and architecture of ancient Egypt were designed to emphasize:

   A. value of the arts in daily life

   B. idea of beauty as seen by the artist

   C. religious idea of eternal life

   D. role of the individual

5) "It is visible from great distances. It is a reminder to all who see it of the wealth and power of the leader of the people who built it, and of his glory and greatness as a god here on Earth."

   The speaker in the passage above is referring to the:

   A. Assyrian king and his lighthouse

   B. Hebrew king and his temple

   C. Egyptian pharaoh and his pyramid

   D. Greek tyrant and the Parthenon

6) Cuneiform and hieroglyphics were important achievements in the development of:

   A. representative government

   B. agricultural production

   C. written language

   D. religious beliefs

EXPLORING WORLD HISTORY

Choose the right answer for each question. Conduct research online as needed

1) The Ten Commandments of the ancient Hebrews influenced development of Western:

    A. moral and ethical teachings   B. feudal social class systems

    C. styles in art and literature   D. parliamentary democracies

2) Jewish scripture says that God's laws were delivered to the Hebrews by:

    A. Abraham   B. Solomon   C. David   D. Moses

3) The diaspora - the dispersing of the Jewish people - refers to:

    A. opposition to the Crusades   B. efforts to convert nonbelievers

    C. a collection of ancient writings   D. exile from their homeland

4) Greece's mountainous terrain and many islands influenced the ancient Greeks to develop:

    A. an economic system based on mining precious metals   B. a political system of independent city-states

    C. a society completely isolated from other civilizations   D. a culture that was uniform throughout its vast empire

5) "We regard an individual who takes no interest in public affairs not as harmless but as useless."
--Pericles' Funeral Oration

The quotation above illustrates the importance ancient Athenians placed on individual participation in the:

    A. education of children   B. economic activities of the household

    C. political process of the city-state   D. religious rituals of the community

6) The legacy of ancient Greek myths and epics, such as the Iliad, provide people with:

    A. objective studies of ancient civilizations   B. real life stories about everyday people

    C. accurate descriptions of historical events   D. heroic figures and great adventures

EXPLORING WORLD HISTORY

Choose the right answer for each question. Conduct research online as needed

1) Atlas, herculean, labyrinth and Olympian are examples of English words that originated in:

A. Greek myths

B. Egyptian hieroglyphics

C. Chinese stories

D. Roman myths

2) Ancient Greeks used myths about their gods primarily to:

A. undermine the Persian religion

B. justify their type of government

C. strike fear in their enemies

D. explain events in the natural world

3) In 480 B.C., Athens and Sparta formed an alliance to fight the:

A. Huns

B. Egyptians

C. Romans

D. Persians

4) How did the rise to power and reign of Alexander most impact Greece?

A. he strengthened democratic rule

B. he established peace with Persia

C. he ended the power of the city-states and unified the nation

D. he made Macedonia the intellectual center of the world

5) An early civilization along the Indus River is in the land later called:

A. Mesopotamia

B. India

C. China

D. Egypt

6) Which statement about the Hindu caste system in India is accurate?

A. foreigners were treated as members of the lowest caste

B. castes were encouraged to interact with one another

C. different castes shared the same rules

D. people were required to remain in the caste they were born in

EXPLORING WORLD HISTORY

Choose the right answer for each question. Conduct research online as needed

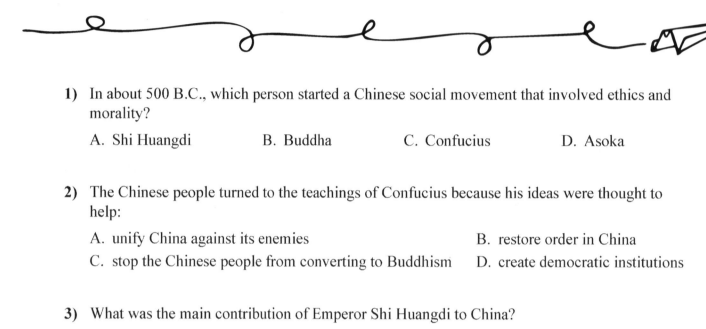

1) In about 500 B.C., which person started a Chinese social movement that involved ethics and morality?

   A. Shi Huangdi   B. Buddha   C. Confucius   D. Asoka

2) The Chinese people turned to the teachings of Confucius because his ideas were thought to help:

   A. unify China against its enemies   B. restore order in China

   C. stop the Chinese people from converting to Buddhism   D. create democratic institutions

3) What was the main contribution of Emperor Shi Huangdi to China?

   A. he unified most of China   B. he required people to speak the Mongol language

   C. he established a public education system in China   D. he encouraged the Hindu religion

SYNONYMS CROSSWORD PUZZLE

Choose the right synonyms to fill in the blanks and complete the puzzle

loquacious	gargantuan	diminutive	redundant
dilemma	surmise	essential	courage
winsome	pallid	predictable	discourteous
ludicrous	frigid	innocuous	tranquil
trifling	remiss	nebulous	revolting

Across →		Down ↓	
4. hazy	**14.** disgusting	**1.** harmless	**9.** impolite
6. repetitive	**17.** problem	**2.** expected	**11.** cold
8. guess	**18.** ridiculous	**3.** bravery	**13.** talkative
10. peaceful	**19.** small	**5.** necessary	**15.** negligent
12. huge	**20.** charming	**7.** unimportant	**16.** pale

19

SYNONYMS CROSSWORD PUZZLE

Choose the right synonyms to fill in the blanks and complete the puzzle

vague	flawless	congenial	compulsory
svelte	terminate	melancholy	expedite
callous	triumph	eccentric	sensitive
ebullient	uniform	disparate	hapless
antagonize	profuse	integrity	futile

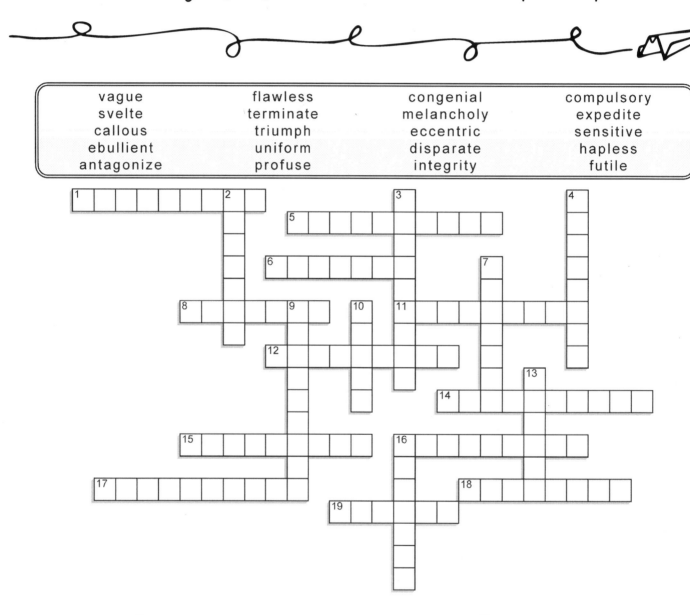

Across →		Down ↓
1. different	**16.** friendly	**2.** succeed
5. sadness	**17.** provoke	**3.** unusual
6. abundant	**18.** hurry	**4.** perfect
8. unfortunate	**19.** thin	**7.** alike
11. end		**9.** touchy
12. honesty		**10.** unclear
14. required		**13.** pointless
15. joyful		**16.** hardened

IDENTIFYING SOLID FIGURES

Determine which type of solid figure is pictured for each

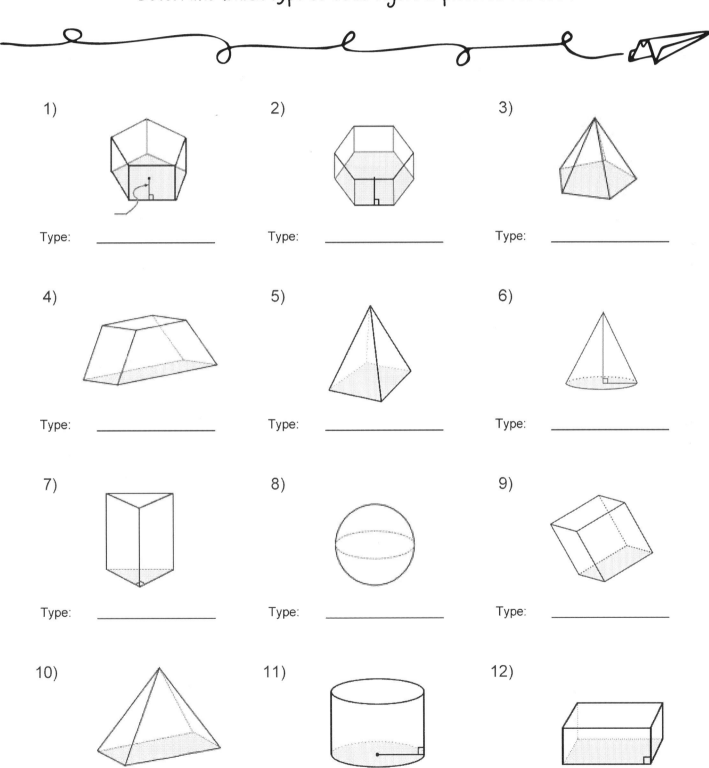

1)

Type: _____

2)

Type: _____

3)

Type: _____

4)

Type: _____

5)

Type: _____

6)

Type: _____

7)

Type: _____

8)

Type: _____

9)

Type: _____

10)

Type: _____

11)

Type: _____

12)

Type: _____

IDENTIFYING SOLID FIGURES

Determine which type of solid figure is pictured for each

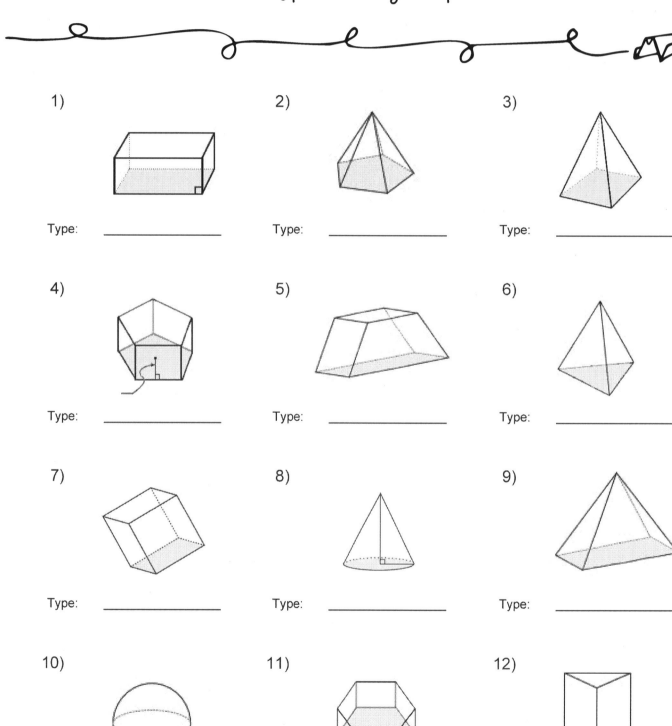

1)

Type: _____

2)

Type: _____

3)

Type: _____

4)

Type: _____

5)

Type: _____

6)

Type: _____

7)

Type: _____

8)

Type: _____

9)

Type: _____

10)

Type: _____

11)

Type: _____

12)

Type: _____

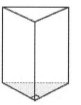

FUN WITH PHYSICS: PROPERTIES OF WAVES

Match each item to the correct definition

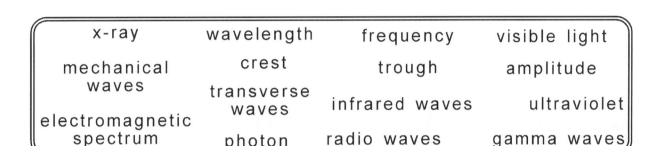

> x-ray   wavelength   frequency   visible light
>
> mechanical waves   crest   trough   amplitude
>
> transverse waves   infrared waves   ultraviolet
>
> electromagnetic spectrum   photon   radio waves   gamma waves

1) tells the intensity of the radiation

2) occurs when the motion of the medium is at right angles to the direction of the wave

3) have the shortest wavelength and the highest frequency

4) the distance between one point of a wave to the same point in the next wave

5) waves used to penetrate solids; they are used in doctor's offices & airports

6) the number of waves per unit of time

7) the top of a wave

8) the bottom of a wave

9) the range of all types of electromagnetic radiation

10) waves that disturb matter

11) tiny particles of light that make up the different forms of waves in the electromagnetic spectrum

12) waves that disturb electromagnetic fields

13) the form of energy we can see (ROYGBIV)

14) waves often used in heat lamps

15) waves used by insects to find nectar; they can also cause sunburn

FUN WITH PHYSICS: PROPERTIES OF WAVES

Match each item to the correct definition

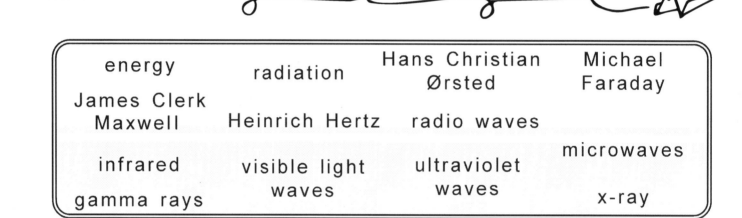

energy	radiation	Hans Christian Ørsted	Michael Faraday
James Clerk Maxwell	Heinrich Hertz	radio waves	microwaves
infrared	visible light waves	ultraviolet waves	
gamma rays			x-ray

1) carries the news and signals to TV and cell phones

2) he proved that you can use magnetism to generate electricity; developed electric motors & generators

3) used in night vision goggles

4) so strong it allows doctors to look at our bones

5) the first person to produce electromagnetic waves in a lab

6) he showed that an electric wire would create a pattern of magnetism

7) visible to the human eye

8) doctors use them to kill diseased cells

9) came up with a theory that explained both electricity and magnetism

10) the sun transmits UV radiation to Earth

11) is the energy that travels and spreads out as it moves

12) power; provides the power to do work

13) heat food, are used for radar images

HEALTH SMARTS: DRUGS & ALCOHOL

Select the appropriate answer for each question

___ 1.   What type of medicine can be purchased without a prescription?

a. Generic medications   b. Over-the-counter medications   c. Antibiotics d. Refills for prescriptions

___ 2.   What are unwanted reactions to a medicine, such as nausea or headaches?

a. Tolerances   b. Withdrawals   c. Side effects   d. Reactions

___ 3.   What is the proper amount of medicine that should be taken at one time?

a. Dose   b. Refill   c. Frequency per day   d. Directions

___ 4.   Suppose someone is taking a medication for a strained back. Once their back is healed they cannot stop taking the medication and when they try to stop they get headaches, chills, and nausea. What type of drug dependence is this?

a. Emotional dependence   b. Physical dependence   c. Psychological dependence   d. Tolerance

___ 5.   If you accidentally take two teaspoons of a medicine instead of one teaspoon it is ____.

a. drug abuse   b. drug use   c. drug misuse   d. drug error

___ 6.   What is the irresistible need to continue a behavior, such as taking drugs, even if it is harmful?

a. Craving   b. Habit   c. Addiction   d. Dependence

___ 7.   What is one of the most important things you can do to maintain a drug-free lifestyle?

a. Accept others who use harmful drugs.   b. Feel confident about hanging out with people who use drugs because you know you will never try them. c. Avoid situations where there are groups of people.   d. Avoid situations where drugs are used.

HEALTH SMARTS: DRUGS & ALCOHOL

Select the appropriate answer for each question

___ 8.   Which of the following is probably NOT a reason that people start abusing drugs?

a. Curiosity   b. Rebellion against parents or guardians   c. Escape from stress d. Positive self-esteem

___ 9.   What is an odorless, colorless, poisonous gas found in tobacco smoke?

a. Hydrogen cyanide   b. Nicotine   c. Hydrogen sulfide   d. Carbon monoxide

___ 10.   A disease in which the lung's air sacs are damaged and cannot fill with oxygen is called ____.

a. cancer   b. bronchitis   c. emphysema   d. smoker's lung

___ 11.   Which addictive substance is absorbed into your bloodstream through tissues in your mouth when you suck or chew tobacco?a. Nicotine

b. Tar   c. Alcohol   d. Cyanide

___ 12.   If someone offers you a cigarette what is the best possible response?

a. "No."   b. "Not now, I just ate."   c. "I'll think about it."   d. "No thanks. I just had one."

___ 13.   At what stage in the path to addiction does tolerance grow as a person uses tobacco at specific times, such as every weekend or every night after dinner?

a. Occasional use   b. Regular use   c. Addiction   d. Social use

___ 14.   What is the thick, sticky fluid produced when tobacco is burned that can coat the lungs?

a. Nicotine   b. Tar   c. Carbon monoxide   d. Charcoal

HEALTH SMARTS: DRUGS & ALCOHOL

Select the appropriate answer for each question

___ 15.   How does cigarette smoking affect a person's skin?

a. It turns skin yellow.   b. It causes lesions on the skin.   c. It ages and wrinkles the skin.   d. It causes melanoma.

___ 16.   What is the most common cause of death from cancer?

a. Exposure to the sun   b. Radiation   c. Smoking   d. Pollution

___ 17.   Exhaled smoke and sidestream smoke from burning tobacco products are called ___.

a. snuff   b. secondhand smoke   c. passive smoke   d. exhaustive smoke

___ 18.   What is a disease in which scar tissues replaces healthy liver cells?

a. Pancreatitis.   b. Diabetes   c. Cirrhosis   d. Sclerosis

___ 19.   The amount of alcohol in a person's blood is their ___.

a. alcohol level   b. blood alcohol content   c. alcohol index   d. alcohol limit

___ 20.   How does alcohol cause a person to have poor judgement?

a. It slows the body's motor functions.   b. It reduces blood flow to the brain.   c. It increases the production of pleasure-causing hormones.   d. It depresses the part of the brain used for reasoning.

___ 21.   What is a disease in which a person is dependent on alcohol?

a. Alcohol syndrome   b. Alcohol dependency   c. Alcoholism   d. Alcohol influence

HEALTH SMARTS: DRUGS & ALCOHOL

Select the appropriate answer for each question

____ 22.   What is a condition that causes birth defects in babies born to mothers who drank alcohol during pregnancy?

a. Fetal alcoholism   b. Infant blood alcohol content   c. Infant alcohol addiction   d. Fetal alcohol syndrome

____ 23.   What type of drug is alcohol?

a. Stimulant   b. Depressant   c. Hallucinogen   d. Narcotic

____ 24.   Drinking alcohol increases the likelihood that you will be involved in ____.

a. healthful behaviors   b. respectful friendships   c. risk behaviors
d. responsible behaviors

____ 25.   What is the best decision to make if someone who has been drinking alcohol offers you a ride home?

a. Refuse the ride and take the person's keys.   b. Refuse the ride and call your parents.   c. Accept the ride since the person did not drink that much. d. Accept the ride since it is your only way to get home.

HEALTH SMARTS: DRUGS & ALCOHOL

Decide whether each statement is true or false

1) (True / False) Drinking alcohol is an effective, long-lasting method for coping with your problems.

2) (True / False) Excessive alcohol consumption can increase your risk of developing certain cancers.

3) (True / False) Vaping is a perfectly healthy alternative to smoking tobacco, since it never has any negative consequences.

4) (True / False) If you simply exercise strong willpower when using drugs, then you won't face any problems with substance abuse.

5) (True / False) Cigarette smoking is the #1 cause of preventable deaths in the United States.

6) (True / False) Chewing tobacco is actually a very safe habit because it doesn't damage your lungs.

7) (True / False) As long as you're not blackout drunk, it's still pretty safe to drive a motor vehicle.

8) (True / False) Although vaping nicotine is less harmful overall than smoking cigarettes, it is still highly addictive.

9) (True / False) Prescription drugs are safe and nothing to worry about, since they're prescribed legally by doctors every single day.

10) (True / False) Cigarette smoke contains a large number of carcinogens -- i.e. substances that can cause cancer in living tissues.

ALL ABOUT WAVES WORD SEARCH

Find all the wave-related chemistry words in the puzzle below

energy	electromagnetic	frequency	amplitude
transverse	longitudinal	wavelength	interference
constructive	destructive	crest	trough
medium	reflection	refraction	diffraction
velocity	radiation	photon	

```
L L O N G I T U D I N A L P Z O M I C P
I N T E R F E R E N C E B E H E G Y N P
G X P L J D I A N C R E D W V O Q F M B
V M N P G Y I H N M V U O I T A T W S E
C G X V H A I O U I T O T T U Q M O E S
U Y D X R I I I T I V C K Q L G J W N H
K X E H W T D C L N U B O S F T P I J L
K L C U A E U P X R R E F L E C T I O N
R J H I M R M D T P M L G W E R F Q C V
P E D B T A F S I R S C T F M Y A V N D
U A F S X J E R O F W A V E L E N G T H
R P N R A D S T E Z F B V D F X W H C L
T O J X A E H V G Q F R E E R K O U R Q
C R U S V C W G O M U T A N L A D K E B
T Y O Q S H T G I O V E C C E O F M S W
Z Y G U J H F I N A L D N E T R C X T T
Z B U L G I O S O G F N J C X I G I T K
G F Y X D H C E K N N Q V B Y P O Y T I
N F P Q S A G T R A N S V E R S E N U Y
U H S K N E L E C T R O M A G N E T I C
```

FILL IN THE BLANKS: WORLD HISTORY

Decide which item best completes each sentence

Marshall Plan	United Nations	Cold War	communism
Korean War	38th parallel	SEATO	Cuban Missile Crisis
NATO	Joseph McCarthy	Khrushchev	

1) The _____ started because communist North Koreans invaded South Korea.

2) The _____ was a long, bitter struggle between the United States and the Soviet Union.

3) After Stalin's death, _____ took control, acting as First Secretary of the Soviet Union's Communist Party.

4) During the 1950's, senator _____ became convinced that communists were trying to take over the U.S. government.

5) The _____ was formed as an organization that would promote global cooperation.

6) The _____ was set up to help Europe recover from WWII.

7) Soviets believed in _____, whereas the Americans believed in democracy.

8) United States troops helped guard the _____ (border zone) between North Korea and South Korea after the Korean War.

9) In 1949, the United States entered a military alliance known as _____.

10) The _____ occurred because Soviets were setting up nuclear missiles in Cuba.

11) _____ was established to protect Southeast Asian countries against the spread of communism.

1-STEP EQUATIONS WITH FRACTIONS

Solve the equations. Round your answers to the nearest hundredth

1) $c + \frac{5}{8} = 7$

2) $\frac{1}{3} = \frac{2}{5} + n$

3) $f + 22\frac{2}{9} = 19$

4) $d + 12 = -11\frac{7}{9}$

5) $26\frac{1}{9} + k = 24$

6) $\frac{2}{9}r = 7$

7) $22\frac{5}{8} = -4\frac{6}{7} + x$

8) $19\frac{8}{9} = 2\frac{5}{7}a$

9) $\frac{2}{9} = v - \frac{7}{8}$

10) $-14\frac{1}{8}b = 25\frac{5}{8}$

1-STEP EQUATIONS WITH FRACTIONS

Solve the equations. Round your answers to the nearest hundredth

1) $29\frac{4}{7} = -12\frac{7}{8} + k$

2) $v - 24\frac{4}{9} = 26$

3) $22\frac{3}{4} = -3\frac{1}{3}b$

4) $\frac{2}{3} = -\frac{1}{9} + h$

5) $4\frac{2}{5} + s = -24\frac{1}{9}$

6) $\frac{4}{7}c = 7$

7) $\frac{2}{3} = a + \frac{1}{5}$

8) $\frac{4}{5} + f = 5$

9) $r - 12 = -20\frac{6}{7}$

10) $y - \frac{2}{5} = 18$

VOCABULARY MATCH GAME

Match each word to the correct definition

postpone	commodities	germinate	bereavement
astute	revive	admirable	ecstasy
unlucky	verbatim	brazen	enunciate
decent	capricious	aquatic	

1) able to figure things or people out

2) great happiness or joy

3) make something grow

4) word for word

5) worthy of praise

6) bold and without shame

7) given to sudden change

8) sadness from a loss or death

9) to speak clearly

10) of the water

11) put off until later

12) proper and respectable

13) things bought or sold

14) bring back to life

15) having bad fortune

VOCABULARY MATCH GAME

Match each word to the correct definition

obvious	ambiguous	ancestor	descendant
frugal	impulsive	charitable	valor
entrust	terrestrial	clarify	overbearing
voluntary	announce	vindicate	

1) giving of time or money

2) done by choice

3) clear or able to be seen

4) domineering in manner

5) open to interpretation

6) great courage in the face of danger

7) family who comes after you

8) family who came before you

9) to make understandable

10) to make known

11) clear of blame

12) put in someone's care

13) acting before thinking

14) careful with money

15) of the earth

EARTH SCIENCE: WEATHER PATTERNS

Supply the right answer for each question. Conduct research online as needed

1. The layer of gases that surrounds Earth is called the _____
2. The two most abundant gases in the atmosphere are _____
3. Water vapor is water in the form of a _____
4. Earth's atmosphere is important to living things because it provides _____
5. Air has pressure because air has _____
6. Instruments used to measure air pressure are called _____
7. The air pressure acting on the roof of your house comes from _____
8. As you rise upwards in the atmosphere, air pressure _____
9. Clouds form when water vapor in the air becomes _____
10. When climbing a high mountain, you get out of breath easily because _____
11. The layer of our atmosphere in which weather occurs is the _____
12. The ozone layer protects living things on Earth from _____
13. Most air pollution comes from burning _____
14. Most of Earth's incoming ultraviolet radiation is absorbed by _____
15. The greenhouse effect is _____
16. The freezing point of pure water on the Celsius scale is _____
17. Heat from the sun reaches you by _____
18. Convection takes place because cold air is more _____
19. Winds are caused by differences in _____
20. Cool air tends to be more dense and flow _____
21. Wind speed is measured by a(n) _____
22. Land breezes occur because land _____
23. Global winds generally blow _____
24. Earth's rotation makes global winds curve. This is called the _____
25. The doldrums are characterized by _____
26. Relative humidity can be measured with a(an) _____
27. Two conditions are required for cloud formation: cooling of the air and _____
28. Large clouds that often produce thunderstorms are called _____
29. Very high feathery clouds are called _____

EARTH SCIENCE: WEATHER PATTERNS

Supply the right answer for each question. Conduct research online as needed

30. Layered clouds that often cover much of the sky and are a dull gray color are called _____

31. Any form of water that falls from clouds is called _____

32. Cold, dry air affecting the northern United States in winter often comes from _____

33. When a rapidly moving cold air mass overtakes a slow-moving warm air mass, the result is a(n) _____

34. When a warm air mass and a cold air mass meet and neither can move the other, the result is a(n) _____

35. A funnel-shaped cloud that touches Earth's surface is called a _____

36. One of the best places to seek protection during a tornado is _____

37. Weather forecasting has improved recently in part because of improved _____

38. Scientists who study weather and try to predict it are called _____

39. Isobars are lines on a map joining places that have the same _____

40. On weather maps, a line with half circles indicates a _____

41. What kind of weather would a continental tropical air mass that formed over northern Mexico bring to the southwestern United States? _____

42. Tornado Alley includes the states of _____

43. Hurricanes typically form over warm _____

44. The eye of a hurricane is _____

45. Which source of weather data would enable a meteorologist to follow the path of an approaching thunderstorm?

_____

46. The prevailing westerlies, the major wind belts over the continental United States, generally push air masses from

_____

47. One example of a safe place to be during a thunderstorm is crouching in _____

48. If people are asked to evacuate during a hurricane watch, they are being asked to _____

49. The cycle of heating, rising, cooling, and sinking is called a _____

50. What is the most abundant gas in air? _____

EARTH SCIENCE: WEATHER PATTERNS

Supply the right answer for each question. Conduct research online as needed

Local Winds

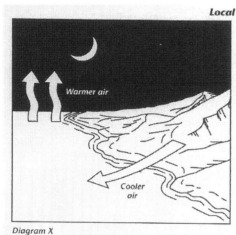

Diagram X

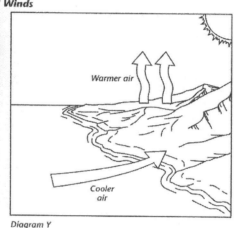

Diagram Y

51. In diagram X, from which way does the wind blow? Land or sea? _____

52. In diagram Y, from which way does the wind blow? Land or sea? _____

53. Which diagram shows the formation of a sea breeze? _____

54. Which diagram shows the formation of a land breeze? _____

55. In diagram X, which cools more quickly, the land or water? _____

Weather Map

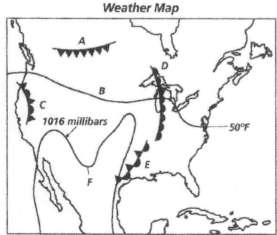

56. What does A represent? In what direction is it moving? _____

57. What is B called? _____

58. What does D represent? In what direction is it moving? _____

59. What does E represent? _____

60. What does F connect? _____

VERBS FOR THE WIN

Identify the correct answer to each question

Question #1:
Write the verb in this sentence.
Landscapers design a plan for the home.

Question #2:
Write the verb in this sentence.
The homeowners approve the drawings for the landscape.

Question #3:
Write the verb in this sentence.
Workers level the yard.

Question #4:
Write the verb in this sentence.
The planting beds require special attention.

Question #5:
Write the linking verb in this sentence.
The flower beds are now ready for planting.

Question #6:
Write the verb in this sentence.
The workers unroll the freshly cut sod.

Question #7:
Write the verb in this sentence.
The homeowners love their beautiful landscaping.

Question #8:
Choose the verb from this group of words.
   A.   happiness
   B.   abandon
   C.   capsule

Question #9:
Choose the verb from this group of words.
   A.   bachelor
   B.   achieve
   C.   stomach

Question #10:
Choose the verb from this group of words.
   A.   insect
   B.   jiggle
   C.   illegal

Question #11:
Choose the verb from this group of words.
   A.   examine
   B.   pirate
   C.   radius

Question #12:
Choose the verb from this group of words.
   A.   worker
   B.   begin
   C.   student

Question #13:
Write the linking verb in this sentence.
My aunt is a school teacher.

Question #14:
Write the linking verb in this sentence.
Marla was a first grade teacher last year.

Question #15:
Write the linking verb in this sentence.
Marla's school looks bright and friendly.

Question #16:
Write the linking verb in this sentence.
Katrina became a sixth grade teacher this year.

Question #17:
Write the linking verb in this sentence.
Valerie's favorite subjects are math and science.

VERBS FOR THE WIN

Identify the correct answer to each question

Question #18:
Write the linking verb in this sentence.
Mrs. Brown's students feel comfortable in her class.

Question #19:
Write the linking verb in this sentence.
Susan seems to really enjoy her job.

Question #20:
Write the linking verb in this sentence.
Miss Davis's principal was pleased with her work.

Question #21:
Write the linking verb in this sentence.
Dana is excited about next year.

Question #22:
Write the linking verb in this sentence.
The school appears empty for the summer.

Question #23:
Write the verb in this sentence.
Work begins shortly after approval.

Question #24:
Write the verb in this sentence.
The landscaper chooses the plants.

Question #25:
Write the verb in this sentence.
Workers place mulch around the plants.

SURFACE AREA: PRISMS & CYLINDERS

Find the surface area of each. Round answers to the nearest hundredth if needed

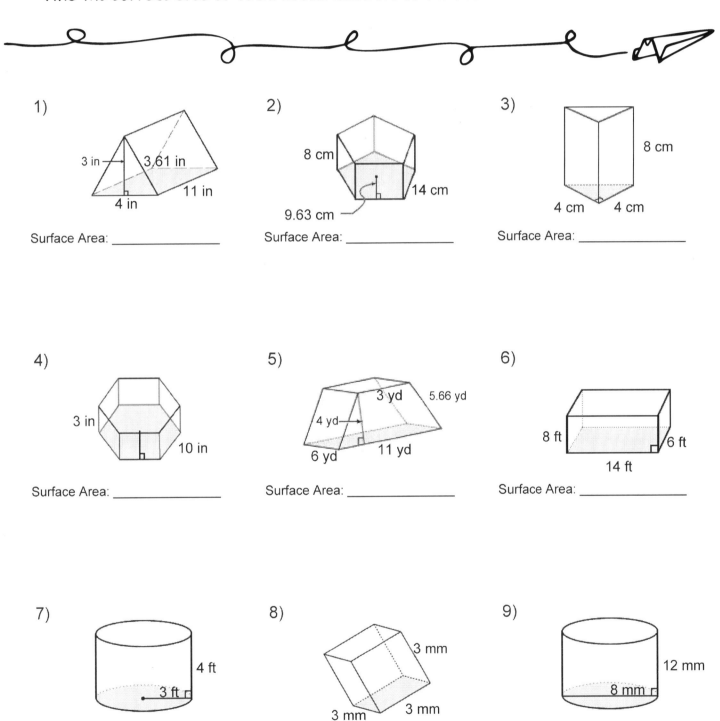

1)

3 in   3.61 in
      11 in
   4 in

Surface Area: _____

2)

8 cm
      14 cm
9.63 cm

Surface Area: _____

3)

8 cm

4 cm   4 cm

Surface Area: _____

4)

3 in
      10 in

Surface Area: _____

5)

3 yd   5.66 yd
4 yd
6 yd   11 yd

Surface Area: _____

6)

8 ft   6 ft
   14 ft

Surface Area: _____

7)

4 ft
3 ft

Surface Area: _____

8)

3 mm
3 mm   3 mm

Surface Area: _____

9)

12 mm
8 mm

Surface Area: _____

SURFACE AREA: PRISMS & CYLINDERS

Find the surface area of each. Round answers to the nearest hundredth if needed

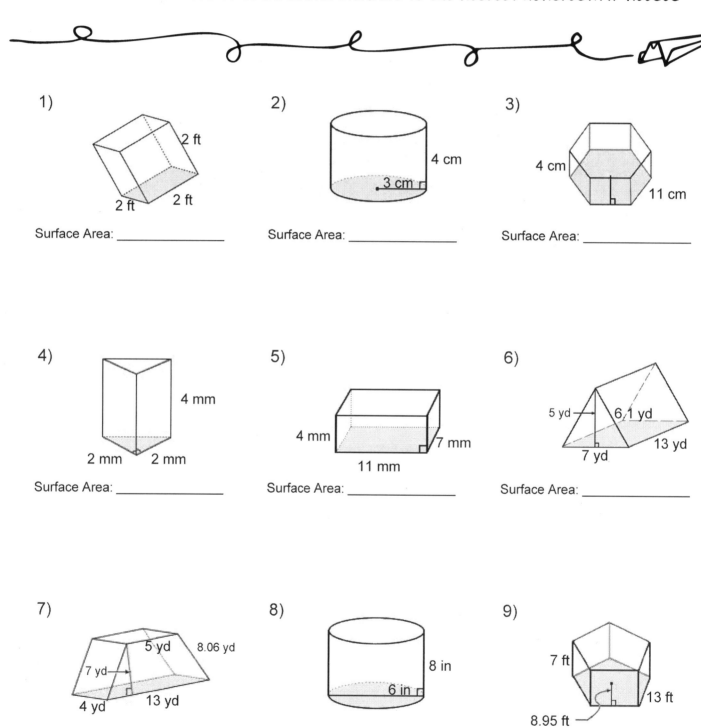

1)

2 ft
2 ft
2 ft

Surface Area: _____

2)

4 cm
3 cm

Surface Area: _____

3)

4 cm
11 cm

Surface Area: _____

4)

4 mm
2 mm   2 mm

Surface Area: _____

5)

4 mm
7 mm
11 mm

Surface Area: _____

6)

5 yd   6.1 yd
7 yd   13 yd

Surface Area: _____

7)

5 yd   8.06 yd
7 yd
4 yd   13 yd

Surface Area: _____

8)

8 in
6 in

Surface Area: _____

9)

7 ft
13 ft
8.95 ft

Surface Area: _____

TRUE OR FALSE: OUTER SPACE EDITION

Decide whether each statement is true or false

1) (True / False) The study of the Moon, planets, stars and other objects in space is known as "astronomy."

2) (True / False) The universal law of gravitation was established by Sir Isaac Newton.

3) (True / False) The Milky Way galaxy is one of billions of galaxies in the known universe.

4) (True / False) The surface of the Moon "shines" because it reflects light from the Sun.

5) (True / False) During a lunar eclipse, the Moon passes through the Earth's shadow.

6) (True / False) The planet Mars is best known for the beautiful rings which encircle its equator.

7) (True / False) A simple pinhole camera can be used to view a solar eclipse safely.

8) (True / False) Neptune is the closest planet to Earth.

9) (True / False) Earth is the only planet in our solar system known to support life.

10) (True / False) The orbits of the planets in our solar system - and of most planetary objects in space - are perfectly circular.

TRUE OR FALSE: OUTER SPACE EDITION

Decide whether each statement is true or false

1) (True / False) The Milky Way is an example of a spiral galaxy.

2) (True / False) The Sun is a star.

3) (True / False) Your weight on the Moon is 20% heavier than what you would experience here on Earth.

4) (True / False) The Sun is mostly made up of hydrogen and helium gases in plasma form.

5) (True / False) A "moon" is a celestial body orbiting a planet or something else that isn't a star.

6) (True / False) Europa is a large moon orbiting Jupiter.

7) (True / False) Pluto was formerly classified as a planet, but is now classified as a dwarf planet instead.

8) (True / False) Contrary to popular belief, the Moon's gravitational pull has no influence on Earth's tides.

9) (True / False) Mercury was the first planet to be discovered via telescope.

10) (True / False) Venus spins in the opposite direction from most other planets, including Earth.

WORLD RELIGIONS CROSSWORD PUZZLE

Choose the right words to fill in the blanks and complete the puzzle

Brahmanism	Buddhism	Christianity	Confucianism
Hinduism	Daoism	religion	Torah
Vedas	monotheism	synagogue	Judaism
Exodus	karma		

Across →

2. the first five books of the Jewish Bible

5. a place of Jewish worship

6. a set of spiritual beliefs, values and practices

8. a major world religion that was founded by the Hebrews

10. an ancient Indian religion in which the Brahmins (priests and religious scholars) are the dominant class

11. a collection of Hindu sacred writings

13. India's first major religion; the third largest religion after Christianity and Islam

14. the belief that there is only one God

Down ↓

1. a Chinese philosophy that emphasizes living in harmony with nature

3. the religion based on the life and teachings of Jesus Christ

4. a Chinese philosophy that emphasizes proper behavior

7. the escape of the Hebrews from Egyptian slavery

9. in Hinduism, the belief that how a person lives will affect their next life

12. a religion of India begun by Prince Siddhartha, or the Buddha

HUMAN CIVILIZATION CROSSWORD PUZZLE

Choose the right words to fill in the blanks and complete the puzzle

aqueduct	civilization	emperor	empire
culture	imperial	republic	irrigation
migration	politics	merchant	settlement

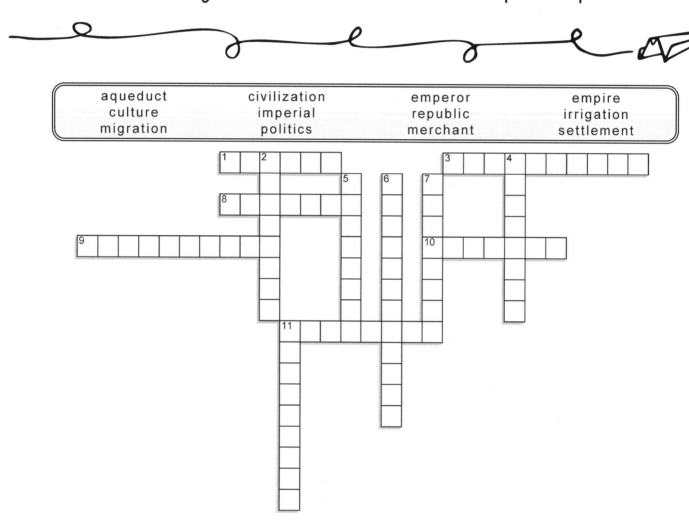

Across →

1. a large territory in which several groups of people are ruled by a single leader or government

3. a means of supplying land with water

8. a characteristic of civilization that includes the beliefs and behaviors of a society or group of people

9. a small community or village

10. the leader of an empire

11. a person who makes money by selling goods

Down ↓

2. having to do with government

4. having to do with an empire

5. a form of government with elected leaders

6. a culture marked by developments in arts, sciences, government and social structure

7. a pipe or channel that brings water from distant places

11. moving from one geographic region to another

GEOGRAPHY & CLIMATE: NATURAL DISASTERS

Supply the correct answer for each question. Conduct research online as needed

1. What are three things needed to triangulate the epicenter of an earthquake?

2. Name three things that can cause tsunamis.

3. What happens as tsunamis move toward shore?

4. What do scientists record to find the epicenter of an earthquake?

5. What is the difference between the epicenter and the focus of an earthquake?

6. Why do earthquakes usually occur at plate boundaries?

7. What should you do if inside during an earthquake?

8. What should you do if inside a car during an earthquake?

9. Describe intensity XII on the Mercalli Scale.

10. How does the ground move under the influence of Rayleigh waves?

GEOGRAPHY & CLIMATE: NATURAL DISASTERS

Supply the correct answer for each question. Conduct research online as needed

11. Name three things that signal a volcanic eruption.

12. What is another name for composite volcanoes?

13. What happens at a convergent boundary when an island arc forms?

14. Which scale most accurately measures a large magnitude earthquake?

15. What happens to buildings during an earthquake?

16. Which magnitude scales express measurements numerically?

17. What is the difference between the Richter and Mercalli Scales?

18. Which type of volcano is made up of pyroclastic material?

19. Name three ways to classify a volcanic eruption.

20. Compare the chemical compositions of mafic and felsic magma.

21. How does the chemical composition of magma affect the explosivity of a volcanic eruption?

GRAPHING INEQUALITIES

Graph the given inequalities

1) $s \leq 9$

0 1 2 3 4 5 6 7 8 9 10 11 12 13 14

2) $s \leq -0.5$

-3 -2 -1 0 1 2 3

3) $3 \leq r$

0 1 2 3 4 5 6 7 8 9 10 11 12 13 14

4) $-b > -1$

-7 -6 -5 -4 -3 -2 -1 0 1 2 3 4 5 6 7

5) $3 > d$

0 1 2 3 4 5 6 7 8 9 10 11 12 13 14

6) $5 \geq w$

0 1 2 3 4 5 6 7 8 9 10 11 12 13 14

7) $-2.5 \leq -f$

-3 -2 -1 0 1 2 3

8) $-j > -1$

-7 -6 -5 -4 -3 -2 -1 0 1 2 3 4 5 6 7

9) $-0.5 \geq -z$

-3 -2 -1 0 1 2 3

10) $13 < a$

0 1 2 3 4 5 6 7 8 9 10 11 12 13 14

11) $p \leq 9$

0 1 2 3 4 5 6 7 8 9 10 11 12 13 14

12) $-z > -4$

-7 -6 -5 -4 -3 -2 -1 0 1 2 3 4 5 6 7

13) $-1.5 \geq -v$

-3 -2 -1 0 1 2 3

14) $2.5 \geq a$

-3 -2 -1 0 1 2 3

15) $10 < k$

0 1 2 3 4 5 6 7 8 9 10 11 12 13 14

16) $-f > 0.5$

-3 -2 -1 0 1 2 3

17) $v \geq -1$

-7 -6 -5 -4 -3 -2 -1 0 1 2 3 4 5 6 7

18) $2 < -g$

-7 -6 -5 -4 -3 -2 -1 0 1 2 3 4 5 6 7

19) $p < -3$

-7 -6 -5 -4 -3 -2 -1 0 1 2 3 4 5 6 7

20) $-n < -2$

-7 -6 -5 -4 -3 -2 -1 0 1 2 3 4 5 6 7

GRAPHING INEQUALITIES

Write inequalities from the given graphs

1) k _____

2) a _____
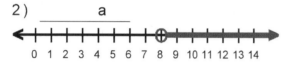

3) w _____

4) f _____
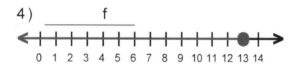

5) f _____
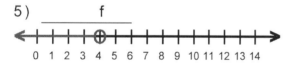

6) z _____
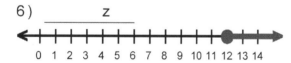

7) h _____
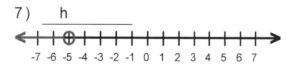

8) c _____

9) y _____

10) g _____
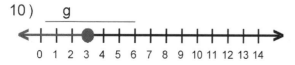

11) w _____

12) b _____

13) y _____

14) w _____
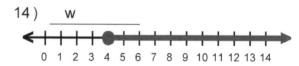

15) c _____
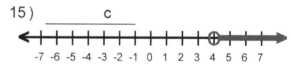

16) k _____

17) h _____
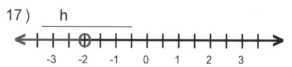

18) z _____
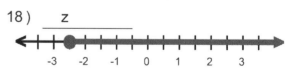

19) a _____
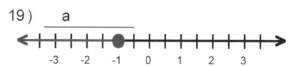

20) k _____
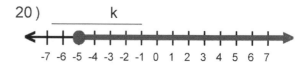

50

ADD & SUBTRACT INEQUALITIES

Solve and graph the inequalities

1) - 10 $\leq$ k + 8

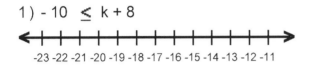

-23 -22 -21 -20 -19 -18 -17 -16 -15 -14 -13 -12 -11

6) 5 $\leq$ g + 9

-9 -8 -7 -6 -5 -4 -3 -2 -1 0 1 2 3

2) y + 3 $<$ 14

7 8 9 10 11 12 13 14 15 16 17 18 19

7) - 7 $\geq$ 6 + h

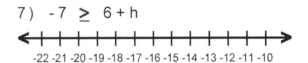

-22 -21 -20 -19 -18 -17 -16 -15 -14 -13 -12 -11 -10

3) - 16 $>$ - 1 + w

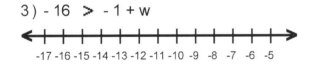

-17 -16 -15 -14 -13 -12 -11 -10 -9 -8 -7 -6 -5

8) 5 $>$ v + 4

-3 -2 -1 0 1 2 3 4 5 6 7 8 9

4) - 5 + q $\geq$ 11

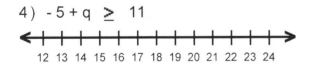

12 13 14 15 16 17 18 19 20 21 22 23 24

9) 4 + a $\leq$ -6

-16 -15 -14 -13 -12 -11 -10 -9 -8 -7 -6 -5 -4

5) - 11 $<$ 6 + z

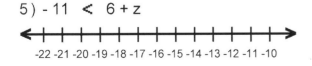

-22 -21 -20 -19 -18 -17 -16 -15 -14 -13 -12 -11 -10

10) 16 $>$ b + 5

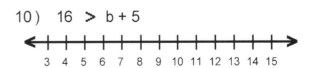

3 4 5 6 7 8 9 10 11 12 13 14 15

ADD & SUBTRACT INEQUALITIES

Solve and graph the inequalities

1)   j - 3 $\geq$ -18

-23 -22 -21 -20 -19 -18 -17 -16 -15 -14 -13 -12 -11

6)   14 $<$ h + 1

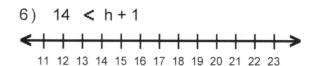
11 12 13 14 15 16 17 18 19 20 21 22 23

2)   x + 3 $\geq$ -15

-25 -24 -23 -22 -21 -20 -19 -18 -17 -16 -15 -14 -13

7) -12 $>$ v - 4

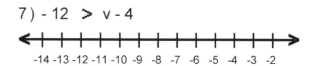
-14 -13 -12 -11 -10 -9 -8 -7 -6 -5 -4 -3 -2

3)   d - 2 $\leq$ 14

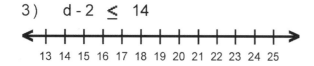
13 14 15 16 17 18 19 20 21 22 23 24 25

8) -10 $\leq$ 3 + k

-22 -21 -20 -19 -18 -17 -16 -15 -14 -13 -12 -11 -10

4)   -6 $<$ w + 5

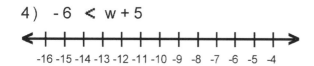
-16 -15 -14 -13 -12 -11 -10 -9 -8 -7 -6 -5 -4

9)   8 + n $\geq$ 18

1 2 3 4 5 6 7 8 9 10 11 12 13

5)   y - 4 $>$ 5

0 1 2 3 4 5 6 7 8 9 10 11 12

10)   7 + s $<$ 5

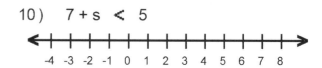
-4 -3 -2 -1 0 1 2 3 4 5 6 7 8

52

LANGUAGE ARTS: SUPER SPELLER QUIZ

Identify the correct spelling of each word

1) A. architectior   B. archetecture   C. architecture   D. archactecture

2) A. enviroment   B. envirement   C. enviorment   D. environment

3) A. disatisfied   B. dissatissfied   C. dissatesfied   D. dissatisfied

4) A. adjourn   B. addjourn   C. adjern   D. adjurn

5) A. authenticaty   B. authenticity   C. athenticity   D. authenticety

6) A. adventure   B. addventure   C. adventior   D. advenshure

7) A. symettry   B. symmatry   C. symmetry   D. symetry

8) A. conservashen   B. consarvation   C. conservashion   D. conservation

9) A. conclussion   B. conclusion   C. conclujen   D. conclushion

10) A. imajination   B. imaginashen   C. imaginashion   D. imagination

11) A. illitaret   B. illiterate   C. illitarate   D. illitterate

12) A. literiture   B. literature   C. litterature   D. litteratur

13) A. amacher   B. ameteur   C. amateur   D. amateure

14) A. defendant   B. deffendent   C. deffendant   D. defendent

15) A. biodegradable   B. biodigradible   C. biodagradable   D. biodegraddable

LANGUAGE ARTS: SUPER SPELLER QUIZ

Identify the correct spelling of each word

1) A. opponent   B. oponant   C. opponnent   D. oponent

2) A. auditoriam   B. auditoriem   C. audatorium   D. auditorium

3) A. dimensionall   B. dimenshional   C. dimmensional   D. dimensional

4) A. signeture   B. signature   C. signacher   D. signiture

5) A. elivator   B. elevator   C. elavator   D. elevater

6) A. commercial   B. commertial   C. comercial   D. commershal

7) A. pollution   B. pollushion   C. polution   D. pollushen

8) A. juditial   B. juddicial   C. judishial   D. judicial

9) A. encyclopedia   B. incyclopedia   C. encyclapedia   D. encyclipedia

10) A. protracter   B. potractor   C. protractor   D. prottractor

11) A. innersecting   B. intorsecting   C. entersecting   D. intersecting

12) A. apprentice   B. aprentise   C. aprentice   D. apprentece

13) A. league   B. laegue   C. leaggue   D. leageu

14) A. librarion   B. librarian   C. librarien   D. libbrarian

15) A. disposable   B. desposible   C. desposable   D. disposible

VERB MASTERY

Identify the correct answer to each question

Question #1:
Read the following sentence and identify the main verb.
The storm approached from the southwest.
  A.   approached
  B.   storm
  C.   southwest

Question #2:
Read the following sentence and identify the main verb.
Leo and Lisa carried in the porch furniture.
  A.   furniture
  B.   carried
  C.   porch

Question #3:
Read the following sentence and identify the main verb.
I attended the judo class on Tuesday.
  A.   judo
  B.   attended
  C.   class

Question #4:
Read the following sentence and identify the main verb.
She passed the test for her green belt.
  A.   test
  B.   belt
  C.   passed

Question #5:
Read the following sentence and identify the main verb.
Her hat appeared too small for her head.
  A.   appeared
  B.   small
  C.   head

Question #6:
Read the following sentence and identify the verb phrase.
When will the magic show begin?
  A.   will begin
  B.   When will begin
  C.   show begin

Question #7:
Read the following sentence and identify the verb phrase.
Norma was taking part in a special kind of race.
  A.   was taking
  B.   special kind
  C.   taking part

Question #8:
Read the following sentence and identify the verb phrase.
The children in the audience are jumping up and down.
  A.   are jumping
  B.   jumping up
  C.   jumping up and down

Question #9:
Read the following sentence and identify the verb phrase.
Both people and horses will be competing.
  A.   will be
  B.   will be competing
  C.   be competing

Question #10:
Read the following sentence and identify the verb phrase.
Gloria has always helped on Saturdays.
  A.   has helped
  B.   has always helped
  C.   has always

Question #11:
Read the following sentence and identify the verb phrase.
Jill will be in the 100-meter race tomorrow.
  A.   will be
  B.   will
  C.   will be in

Question #12:
Read the following sentence and identify the verb phrase.
The rabbits have been sitting in the cage all day.
  A.   have been
  B.   have been sitting
  C.   been sitting

Question #13:
Read the following sentence and identify the verb phrase.
She will carefully ride the horse to the barn.
  A.   carefully ride
  B.   will ride
  C.   will carefully ride

VERB MASTERY

Identify the correct answer to each question

Question #14:
Read the following sentence and identify the verb phrase.
The youngest dolphins are watching the other two.
- A. watching the
- B. dolphins are
- C. are watching

Question #15:
Read the following sentence and identify the verb.
The dolphins should all swim to the side of the pool.
- A. should all
- B. should swim
- C. should all swim

Question #16:
Identify the words in this sentence that could make a contraction.
She was not sure if she was staying at home.
- A. not sure
- B. was not
- C. was staying

Question #17:
Identify the words in this sentence that could make a contraction.
If she cannot go this year, maybe she can go next year.
- A. can go
- B. cannot
- C. maybe she

Question #18:
Identify the words in this sentence that could make a contraction.
Who would not want to go to Marvel Mountain?
- A. would not
- B. would want
- C. go to

Question #19:
Identify the words in this sentence that could make a contraction.
We have not had a chance to discuss our plans.
- A. not had
- B. chance to
- C. have not

Question #20:
Identify the words in this sentence that could make a contraction.
She will want to join us when she hears our plans.
- A. will want
- B. She will
- C. want to

Question #21:
Read the following sentence and identify the main verb.
John crushed the tin cans with his foot.
- A. crushed
- B. cans
- C. tin

Question #22:
Read the following sentence and identify the main verb.
Lewis quickly ties bundles of newspapers.
- A. bundles
- B. ties
- C. quickly

Question #23:
Read the following sentence and identify the main verb.
Everyone admires her skill and bravery.
- A. bravery
- B. admires
- C. skill

Question #24:
Read the following sentence and identify the main verb.
Dr. Smith saved my hamster's life.
- A. saved
- B. hamster's
- C. life

Question #25:
Read the following sentence and identify the main verb.
Next week the new emergency clinic opens.
- A. emergency
- B. new
- C. opens

CHEMISTRY MATCH GAME

Match each item to the correct definition

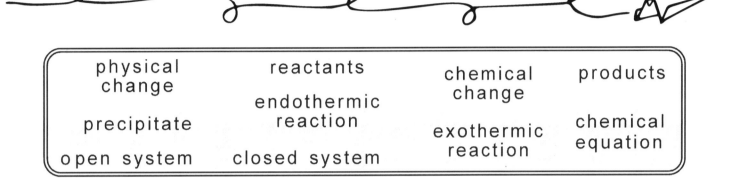

physical change	reactants	chemical change	products
precipitate	endothermic reaction	exothermic reaction	chemical equation
open system	closed system		

1) a change that alters the form or appearance of a substance but does not change it into another substance

2) tells you the substances you start with in a reaction, as well as the substances that are formed at the end of the reaction

3) a solid that forms from liquids undergoing chemical changes in a chemical reaction

4) matter does not enter or leave (e.g. a closed bottle)

5) substances that undergo chemical changes

6) matter can enter form or escape (e.g. an open fish bowl)

7) net energy is released from a chemical reaction (usually this energy is heat)

8) a change that produces one or more new substances

9) net energy is required for the chemical reaction to take place

10) the newly formed substances that result from a chemical change

CHEMISTRY MATCH GAME

Match each item to the correct definition

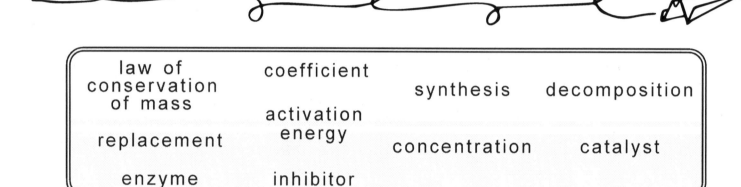

law of conservation of mass	coefficient	synthesis	decomposition
replacement	activation energy	concentration	catalyst
enzyme	inhibitor		

1) the minimum amount of energy needed to start a chemical reaction

2) a material used to decrease the rate of a chemical reaction (e.g. food preservatives)

3) increases the reaction rate by lowering the activation energy needed

4) reaction where one element replaces another in a compound

5) states that during a chemical reaction, matter is not created or destroyed

6) number placed in front of a chemical formula in an equation

7) the amount of a substance in a given volume

8) a type of biological catalyst (e.g. digestive enzymes in the human body)

9) reaction when 2 or more elements or compounds combine to form a more complex substance/product

10) reaction when a compound breaks down into 2 or more simpler products

VOLCANIC STUDIES WORD SEARCH

Find all the volcano-related terms in the word search below

earthquakes	volcanoes	epicenter	magnitude
mid-ocean ridge	shadow zone	intensity	subduction zone
pyroclastic material	focus	magma	pillow lava
seismology	hot spot	elastic rebound	pahoehoe
caldera	convection		

```
A  C  R  E  V  O  L  C  A  N  O  E  S  S  Z  X  W  F  I  G
S  U  H  Q  A  F  Z  Y  M  E  D  A  A  H  S  P  V  W  N  K
U  M  E  R  V  R  K  W  O  S  V  F  X  A  A  Q  G  E  I  C
B  L  A  N  E  P  T  H  B  A  D  H  Y  D  K  J  M  P  M  Z
D  H  O  G  G  U  E  H  L  V  A  L  N  O  Z  Q  A  I  H  S
U  O  F  D  N  O  I  W  Q  R  Q  B  O  W  Z  U  G  C  N  K
C  T  M  O  H  I  O  C  E  U  L  U  T  Z  Y  J  M  E  V  S
T  S  Y  A  C  L  T  D  B  A  A  R  M  O  F  D  A  N  Z  G
I  P  P  U  L  U  L  U  O  R  I  K  Y  N  X  E  M  T  D  W
O  O  X  I  V  A  S  U  D  E  Q  R  E  E  L  I  W  E  P  C
N  T  P  Y  C  H  I  Z  U  E  K  S  A  S  T  C  L  R  V  D
Z  P  Y  R  O  C  L  A  S  T  I  C  M  A  T  E  R  I  A  L
O  C  O  N  V  E  C  T  I  O  N  O  E  L  C  W  M  N  S  F
N  X  P  F  Z  I  N  T  E  N  S  I  T  Y  R  W  U  I  H  D
E  C  P  L  A  O  X  Q  V  S  E  I  S  M  O  L  O  G  Y  K
H  C  F  R  E  P  D  W  B  I  L  X  Z  J  S  K  Q  M  N  O
U  K  Q  I  J  A  Y  M  C  O  X  R  V  E  G  Z  H  F  L  N
Y  K  H  G  L  Q  V  A  I  Z  E  N  J  F  M  S  T  U  O  P
M  I  D  O  C  E  A  N  R  I  D  G  E  U  B  I  V  A  O  T
I  D  L  X  B  O  E  L  A  S  T  I  C  R  E  B  O  U  N  D
```

EQUIVALENT RATIOS

Fill in the blanks to complete each row of equivalent ratios

1) $3 : 8 = 6 : \_\_ = 9 : \_\_ = 12 : \_\_ = 15 : \_\_ = 18 : \_\_$

2) $1 : 2 = \_\_ : 4 = 3 : \_\_ = 4 : \_\_ = \_\_ : 10 = 6 : \_\_$

3) $1 : 4 = 2 : \_\_ = \_\_ : 12 = \_\_ : 16 = \_\_ : 20 = 6 : \_\_$

4) $1 : 10 = \_\_ : 20 = \_\_ : 30 = 4 : \_\_ = 5 : \_\_ = 6 : \_\_$

5) $2 : 5 = 4 : \_\_ = 6 : \_\_ = \_\_ : 20 = 10 : \_\_ = 12 : \_\_$

6) $2 : 9 = 4 : \_\_ = 6 : \_\_ = \_\_ : 36 = 10 : \_\_ = \_\_ : 54$

7) $1 : 3 = 2 : \_\_ = 3 : \_\_ = 4 : \_\_ = \_\_ : 15 = \_\_ : 18$

8) $2 : 7 = 4 : \_\_ = 6 : \_\_ = \_\_ : 28 = \_\_ : 35 = 12 : \_\_$

9) $1 : 6 = \_\_ : 12 = \_\_ : 18 = 4 : \_\_ = 5 : \_\_ = 6 : \_\_$

10) $1 : 3 = 2 : \_\_ = \_\_ : 9 = \_\_ : 12 = 5 : \_\_ = \_\_ : 18$

EQUIVALENT RATIOS

Fill in the blanks to complete each row of equivalent ratios

1) 36 : 45 = __ : 10 = __ : 25 = __ : 5 = 40 : __ = __ : 15

2) 9 : 36 = 2 : __ = 5 : __ = __ : 4 = __ : 40 = 3 : __

3) 9 : 72 = __ : 16 = 5 : __ = __ : 8 = 10 : __ = 3 : __

4) 18 : 63 = __ : 14 = __ : 35 = __ : 7 = 20 : __ = __ : 21

5) 18 : 45 = 4 : __ = __ : 25 = __ : 5 = 20 : __ = __ : 15

6) 18 : 27 = __ : 6 = __ : 15 = __ : 3 = 20 : __ = 6 : __

7) 36 : 81 = __ : 18 = __ : 45 = 4 : __ = 40 : __ = 12 : __

8) 9 : 27 = 2 : __ = 5 : __ = __ : 3 = __ : 30 = 3 : __

9) 9 : 18 = __ : 4 = __ : 10 = __ : 2 = __ : 20 = __ : 6

10) 45 : 54 = 10 : __ = 25 : __ = 5 : __ = __ : 60 = 15 : __

GEOLOGY & EARTH SCIENCE

Provide the correct answer for each question. Conduct research online as needed

Compare and contrast the Earth's crust, mantle, and core including temperature, density, and composition.

1. Describe the state of matter and composition of the mantle (for all 3 layers).

2. Which layer of earth is made up of tectonic plates?
3. How do we know what the inside of the earth looks like and what it is made of?

4. What happens to the earth's pressure the deeper you go into the earth?
5. _____ is responsible for making the earth's magnetic field.
6. The core is mostly made up of _____ & _____
7. Describe the difference between the core and the mantle in terms of temperature and density:

Investigate the contribution of minerals to rock composition.

8. What are minerals made of?
9. What do all minerals have in common?

10. True or False: Minerals are or once were organic.
11. Define the following terms as they relate to minerals:
Streak:
Luster:
Cleavage:
Fracture:

GEOLOGY & EARTH SCIENCE

Provide the correct answer for each question. Conduct research online as needed

Mineral	Hardness	Way it breaks	Luster	Streak	Color
Galena	2.5	cleavage	metallic	gray-black	silver, gray
Magnetite	6	fracture	metallic	black	black
Hematite	6	fracture	metallic-dull	red-brown	red-brown, silver, black

12. *Use the chart above to answer this question:* Susan wants to identify a dark, heavy mineral sample she found in the classroom collection. She notices there are three minerals in a chart in a reference book that might match her sample. Susan next observes that her sample mineral has flat, reflective surfaces that break into boxlike steps. She infers the mineral may be galena. If she is correct, one more test will verify her inference. Which property would to best for her to observe next?

Classify rocks by their process of formation.

13. What is the difference between intrusive and extrusive?

14. How do each of the following rock types form?
Sedimentary:
Metamorphic:
Igneous:
15. Why do some igneous rocks have holes?
16. Tell about the traits that are unique to each type of rock:
Sedimentary:
Metamorphic:
Igneous:

Explain the effects of physical processes (plate tectonics, erosion, deposition, volcanic eruption, gravity) on geological features including oceans (composition, currents, and tides).

17. Tectonic plates are found in which layer of earth?
18. Why was Alfred Wegener's idea of continental drift not accepted?

19. What is subduction?

GEOLOGY & EARTH SCIENCE

Provide the correct answer for each question. Conduct research online as needed

20. Where can we see the results of plate movement?

21. What is the MAIN reason that the continents look very different than they did 100 million years ago?

22. Convection Currents cause the movement of
23. What evidence supports the theory of continental drift?

24. What geographic force forms u-shaped valleys?
25. On a topographical map there are curved contour lines that make complete, concentric loops that get smaller and smaller. What is inside the smallest loop?
26. A contour interval
(Use the picture to the right to answer the questions #27-29)
27. What is the elevation of the star?
28. Which letter represents a steep slope?
29. What is the contour interval for this topographical map?
30. What force causes sediments to be moved from one area to another?

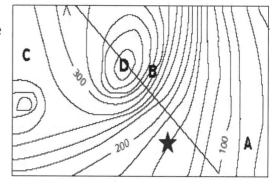

Describe soil as consisting of weathered rocks and decomposed organic material.

31. True or False: Organic Matter is made of sand, silt, & clay, does not help plants grow, and is the only ingredient in soil
32. What is humus?
33. Where does soil get its nutrients?
34. Humus is found in which layer of soil?
35. What is leaching?

GEOLOGY & EARTH SCIENCE

Provide the correct answer for each question. Conduct research online as needed

Students will describe various sources of energy, as well as their uses and conservation.

36. What is conservation?
37. Define biomass
38. What is alternative energy? Name the different types of alternative energy.

39. I am used mainly in the western US. My energy comes from the heat within the Earth. I can be used for home heating. Water that is piped down to me is turned into steam used to turn turbines and generate energy. What am I?

Identify renewable and nonrenewable resources.

40. Which of these items was made from a nonrenewable resource? Paper bag, motor oil, cotton shirt, wooden table
41. What is the difference between a renewable and a recyclable resource?

42. How can having more people on earth impact our use of fossil fuels?

43. How are fossil fuels formed?

44. Natural gas, oil, and coal are all known as

COSMOS MATCH GAME

Match each item to the correct definition

> astronaut Earth Mars star lunar International Space Station
> the Moon Milky Way Neptune
> research Saturn energy the Sun
> the universe Venus solar system Mercury

1) contains the Sun and all the planets that orbit the Sun

2) our closest neighboring planet

3) this orbits the Earth 16 times per day

4) huge ball of burning gas held together by its own gravity

5) orbits the Earth once every 28 days

6) someone who travels in space

7) our home planet

8) power; the ability to do work

9) the center of our solar system

10) the planet closest to the Sun

11) the second planet from the Sun

12) used to describe anything relating to the Moon

13) to study and observe something to learn more about it

14) the 6th planet from the Sun; is known for its rings

15) everything that exists anywhere on Earth or in space

16) the name of our galaxy

17) the 8th planet from the Sun

COSMOS MATCH GAME

Match each item to the correct definition

technology	space	galaxy	comet dust
meteor showers	comet	moon phases	satellite
meteorite	asteroid	asteroid belt	terrestrial planets
astronomical unit	ellipses	Titan	Oort cloud

1) a meteoroid that reaches Earth's surface

2) everything beyond the Earth's atmosphere; where the Sun, stars & other planets are

3) occur when Earth passes through a comet's orbital debris

4) science as it is put to use in the work of everyday life

5) the dust coming off a comet which forms a dust tail

6) a huge collection of comets that completely surrounds the solar system

7) the largest moon in our solar system

8) stars and solar systems grouped together

9) a natural or artificial body revolving around a planet

10) a small rocky body revolving around the Sun

11) a small body of ice, rock and cosmic dust orbiting the Sun

12) is the average distance between the Earth and the Sun

13) are the rocky planets of the inner solar system

14) stretched out circles; describes all orbits

15) occur when the Moon is between the Sun and Earth

16) lies between the orbits of Mars and Jupiter

FIND THE VOLUME: PRISMS & PYRAMIDS

Determine the volume of each. Round answers to the nearest hundredth if needed

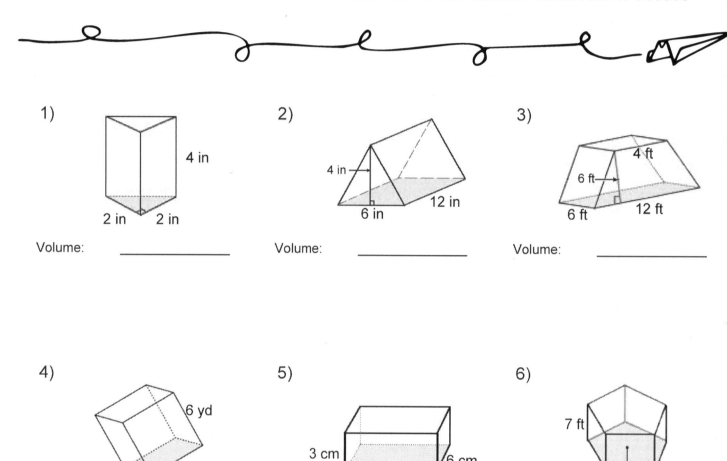

1) 4 in, 2 in, 2 in

Volume: _____

2) 4 in, 6 in, 12 in

Volume: _____

3) 4 ft, 6 ft, 6 ft, 12 ft

Volume: _____

4) 6 yd, 6 yd, 6 yd

Volume: _____

5) 3 cm, 6 cm, 10 cm

Volume: _____

6) 7 ft, 13 ft

Volume: _____

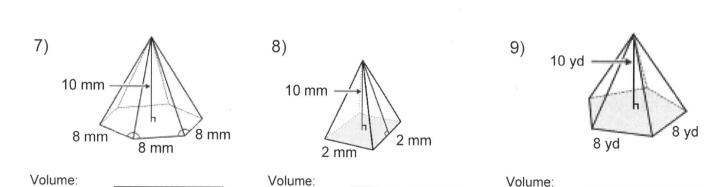

7) 10 mm, 8 mm, 8 mm, 8 mm, 8 mm

Volume: _____

8) 10 mm, 2 mm, 2 mm

Volume: _____

9) 10 yd, 8 yd, 8 yd

Volume: _____

FIND THE VOLUME: PRISMS & PYRAMIDS

Determine the volume of each. Round answers to the nearest hundredth if needed

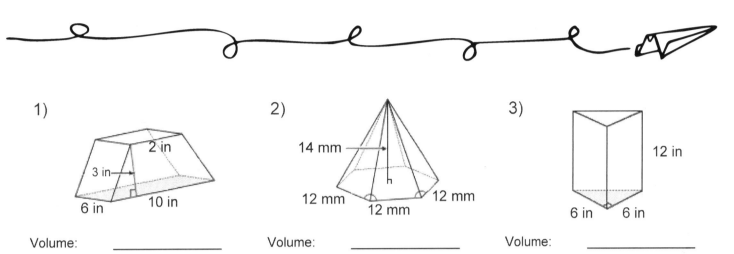

1)

2 in
3 in
6 in
10 in

Volume: _____

2)

14 mm
12 mm
12 mm
12 mm

Volume: _____

3)

12 in
6 in   6 in

Volume: _____

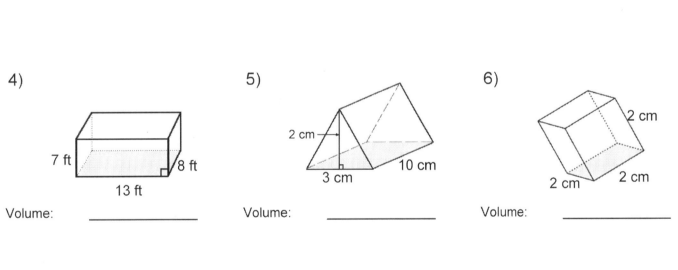

4)

7 ft
8 ft
13 ft

Volume: _____

5)

2 cm
3 cm
10 cm

Volume: _____

6)

2 cm
2 cm
2 cm

Volume: _____

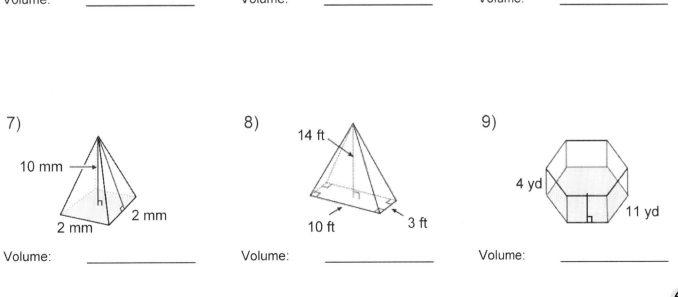

7)

10 mm
2 mm
2 mm

Volume: _____

8)

14 ft
10 ft   3 ft

Volume: _____

9)

4 yd
11 yd

Volume: _____

69

ANCIENT ROME WORD SEARCH

Find all the historical terms in the word search below

Alps	plebeian	patrician	republic
Twelve Tables	Forum	Punic Wars	Pax Romana
gladiators	Colosseum	aqueducts	Christianity
Bible	Rome	Carthage	Julius Caesar
Cleopatra	Augustus	Constantine	Diocletian
Jesus			

```
P  Z  I  J  G  A  K  X  Q  D  F  O  V  N  T  U  B  S  E  N
X  Z  Y  T  H  C  A  R  T  H  A  G  E  Q  O  G  T  V  A  R
W  C  U  Y  W  P  A  T  R  I  C  I  A  N  R  C  E  I  T  A
C  R  O  M  E  E  K  G  B  U  J  R  X  E  U  L  T  O  N  M
N  H  J  Z  Y  A  L  P  J  E  S  U  S  D  B  E  X  A  B  N
R  Q  R  N  G  X  H  V  T  I  Y  B  E  I  L  J  M  E  A  W
J  T  B  I  G  L  C  H  E  M  A  U  B  C  D  O  F  I  S  Y
R  F  H  V  S  C  C  J  Z  T  Q  R  O  N  R  P  E  S  G  U
D  G  F  I  Z  T  L  O  N  A  A  I  E  X  K  B  A  V  Q  Y
W  L  J  H  L  D  I  C  N  R  D  B  A  P  E  G  L  N  E  Q
C  A  M  H  N  Y  O  A  L  S  L  P  L  L  U  J  P  D  A  E
O  D  Y  J  Z  R  A  P  N  E  T  G  P  E  U  B  S  T  X  I
L  I  W  H  C  A  N  F  R  I  O  A  G  K  S  I  L  O  Q  D
O  A  A  U  G  U  S  T  U  S  P  N  G  L  T  H  I  C  E
S  T  N  K  W  T  I  Y  Q  D  A  Y  A  T  F  H  J  L  C  Z
S  O  Y  C  S  T  V  Q  L  M  B  Z  I  T  K  N  X  A  O
E  R  J  U  L  I  U  S  C  A  E  S  A  R  R  N  N  W  M  Q
U  S  P  Y  R  M  W  A  C  S  D  T  Z  K  H  A  E  Q  O  V
M  J  Z  F  U  Q  X  N  W  H  L  B  I  V  Y  P  G  E  R  C
F  O  R  U  M  Y  S  P  U  N  I  C  W  A  R  S  J  W  P  N
```

SCIENCE DEEP DIVE

Supply the correct answer for each question. Conduct research online as needed

Nature of Science

1. What is the difference between an experiment and an investigation?

2. Provide one example of an experiment.

3. Are steps of the scientific inquiry always the same?

4. What is an example of a scientific observation?

5. What is an example of analyzing data?

6. What is a variable?

7. What is a procedure?

8. What is a model? Provide one example.

9. Provide an example of an activity that would be considered scientific?

SCIENCE DEEP DIVE

Supply the correct answer for each question. Conduct research online as needed

10. Define scientific theory.

11. Provide an example of a scientific law.

12. What makes scientific results credible?

13. Why would a map not be a good model of Earth?

Our Planet-Earth

14. How does Earth's surface get energy?

15. List the 5 spheres on Earth?

16. A glacier is an example of what type of sphere?

17. How does water vapor enter the atmosphere?

SCIENCE DEEP DIVE

Supply the correct answer for each question. Conduct research online as needed

18. When the hydrosphere and the atmosphere work together, what are they creating?

19. Which two of Earth's spheres are involved in the water cycle?

20. What would happen if there was no ozone layer present in the atmosphere?

21. Which one of Earth's spheres involves water evaporation?

Weathering and Soil

22. Acid rain is an example of what type of weathering?

Erosion and Deposition

23. Which agent of erosion would cause sinkholes?

24. Which type of landform is created by glacial erosion?

SCIENCE DEEP DIVE

Supply the correct answer for each question. Conduct research online as needed

Weather

25. What is the difference between weather and climate?

26. What happens to air pressure as you move to a higher elevation?

27. What happens when altitude increase?

Climate

28. Which climate factor would affect hurricane movement?

29. Which climate has the fastest rate of weathering?

Energy and Energy Transformations

30. What is the difference between kinetic and potential energy?

31. When would a roller coaster have the most potential energy?

SCIENCE DEEP DIVE

Supply the correct answer for each question. Conduct research online as needed

32. Provide one example of potential energy transforming into kinetic energy?

33. What happens when two like magnets are brought closer to one another?

34. If something is about to fall, what is the change in the amounts of energy?

35. Define the term convection.

Motion and Forces

36. Define the term friction and provide an example.

37. Define the term unbalanced force. Provide one example.

38. Define the term contact force.

39. Create a graph that shows the speed of an object staying constant.

SCIENCE DEEP DIVE

Supply the correct answer for each question. Conduct research online as needed

40. Define the term constant speed.

41. What is the difference between weight and mass?

42. What would happen to the weight of a person if gravity disappeared on Earth?

43. Which type of graph would you use if your data is in the form of percentages?

Classifying and Exploring Life

44. What are the two parts of a scientific name?

45. Why would animals be classified under the same genus name?

46. Define the term dichotomous key? Why is it important?

SCIENCE DEEP DIVE

Supply the correct answer for each question. Conduct research online as needed

Cell Structure and Function

47. Define the term cell.

48. What are the 3 principles of the Cell Theory?

49. What are the difference between plant cells and animal cells?

50. A large animal is made of how many cells? (Think big)

51. Which organelle makes food?

52. Which organelle is responsible for making proteins?

53. What is the purpose of a lysosome?

From a Cell to an Organism

54. Write out the levels of organization.

SCIENCE DEEP DIVE

Supply the correct answer for each question. Conduct research online as needed

Human Body Systems

55. What is the purpose of the respiratory system?

56. Which two body systems work together in order to produce adrenaline?

57. Which two body systems work together to ensure that oxygen gets to all the cells in the body?

Bacteria and Viruses

58. What is the #1 way to protect yourself from infectious diseases?

59. Why are viruses so dangerous to other organisms?

60. Can an antibiotic kill a virus? Explain.

ALGEBRAIC EXPRESSIONS: EVALUATE 1 VARIABLE

Simplify the algebraic expressions

1) -2(5d - 7)   use   d = 5

6) k + 9k   use   k = 4

2) 8x - 9 + 4x   use   x = 8

7) 8k - 7k + 5 - 3   use   k = 9

3) $-\dfrac{15}{c} - 9$ use   c = 5

8) 7f - 2(8 - 3f)   use   f = 8

4) $-\dfrac{s}{8} + 8$ use   s = 16

9) 5(6k - 9) + 2   use   k = 5

5) $3 + \dfrac{h}{8} - 8h$ use   h = 32

10) -8c + 9 - 3 + 2c   use   c = 5

ALGEBRAIC EXPRESSIONS: EVALUATE 1 VARIABLE

Simplify the algebraic expressions

1) 5x + x   use x = 2

2) $\frac{-8}{z}$ + 6 + 2z   use z = -4

3) $\frac{c}{2}$ - 9   use c = 8

4) 4w + 5w   use w = -3

5) 2 - 6f - 4   use f = -8

6) 3 + 2k + 8k   use k = 6

7) 2 + 6 + 3w - 8w   use w = -8

8) -7d + 2(-6d - 9)   use d = 3

9) 2 - $\frac{s}{6}$ use s = 12

10) -8h - 2 + 3 + 5h   use h = 9

MINERAL MATTERS

Provide the correct answer for each question. Conduct research online as needed

1. What kind of minerals do we use in materials like fireworks, cement and building stones?

2. Why would a metal like steel not be a mineral?

3. The evaporation of what liquid leaves behind minerals such as halite and gypsum?

4. What two groups are minerals divided into?

5. What is the range used to measure hardness on the Moh's hardness scale?

6. What would be some examples of native elements?

7. Why are your teeth not considered to be a mineral?

8. In the mineral $CaCO_3$, what does the C stand for?   What does the Ca stand for?
    What does the O stand for?

9. What is a naturally formed, inorganic solid with a definite internal geometric structure called?

10. On the Moh's mineral hardness scale, what would be a soft mineral?

11. Gold, silver and copper are all examples of what?

12. What is more reliable than a minerals color for mineral identification?

13. What is mass divided by volume?

14. Luster can be described in what three categories?

15. What special property only applies to a few minerals?

16. Why would a cake not be considered a mineral?

17. What can be said of rocks and minerals?

MINERAL MATTERS

Provide the correct answer for each question. Conduct research online as needed

18. Where would small crystals form due to slow cooling of hot magma beneath the Earth's crust?

19. Why are gold and silver elements?

20. What is the name given to minerals that contain combinations of carbon and oxygen?

21. What is the property called of minerals for them to tend to break along flat surfaces?

22. What color is quartz in its purest form?

23. What are the two most abundant elements in the Earth's crust?

24. What physical property of minerals can be expressed in numbers?

25. What ore do we get aluminum from?

26. Are mineral ores renewable or nonrenewable resources?

27. What property of minerals do gem cutters take advantage to cut diamonds and rubies?

28. What mineral makes up about half the Earth's crust?

29. When quartz breaks it creates what type of pattern?

30. What are minerals called that are composed of only one element?

31. What are gems?

32. How are minerals most commonly classified?

33. What is the color of the powder a mineral leaves behind on a piece of white, unglazed porcelain?

RENAISSANCE & BEYOND WORD SEARCH

Find all the history terms in the word search below

Renaissance   Humanism   95 Theses   Protestants
Reformation   Lorenzo de Medici   Petrarch   Michelangelo
Leonardo da Vinci   Copernicus   Martin Luther   Johannes Gutenberg
William Shakespeare   King Henry VIII   Galileo

```
H  N  P  U  E  V  C  A  M  K  I  5  Q  W  O  G  F  R  L  X
L  R  Z  Q  B  N  J  E  M  U  T  X  A  F  S  I  K  L  9  D
W  Z  Q  M  V  I  E  H  G  K  X  L  A  J  9  5  R  O  U  P
K  I  C  K  I  N  G  H  E  N  R  Y  V  I  I  I  G  R  V  N
Z  N  L  W  G  Y  D  L  I  M  J  H  E  E  H  R  O  E  O  9
5  X  M  L  L  P  N  D  R  E  C  I  C  F  E  E  Q  N  L  B
G  H  A  5  I  F  B  J  O  R  Z  N  V  B  L  O  9  Z  E  S
S  T  R  R  9  A  5  K  A  L  A  P  N  I  L  C  Z  O  O  C
T  H  T  Q  C  G  M  R  N  S  J  E  L  E  M  O  P  D  N  Y
F  E  I  P  9  5  T  S  S  O  T  A  G  V  G  P  U  E  A  X
Q  Z  N  R  R  E  B  I  H  U  G  N  A  C  L  E  E  M  R  T
E  Q  L  H  P  O  A  Z  G  A  A  L  D  F  S  R  Y  E  D  J
N  Y  U  E  U  N  T  S  I  L  K  M  C  E  T  N  W  D  O  F
C  H  T  N  E  M  E  E  E  M  A  E  S  Y  Q  I  L  I  D  I
V  L  H  R  Z  N  A  H  S  X  Q  E  S  E  N  C  9  C  A  P
9  O  E  A  N  M  C  N  U  T  H  Y  G  P  F  U  B  I  V  P
V  A  R  A  O  I  I  B  I  T  A  G  H  Z  E  S  C  X  I  N
Z  D  H  X  M  L  N  K  5  S  C  N  Y  T  F  A  M  O  N  G
E  O  N  O  9  X  S  9  K  P  M  G  T  C  D  M  R  T  C  R
J  R  E  F  O  R  M  A  T  I  O  N  P  S  M  B  X  E  I  V
```

VERB ROUNDUP

Identify the correct answer to each question

Question #1:
Write the present perfect tense of the capitalized word.
Mother WASHES her hands.

Question #2:
Write the present perfect tense of the capitalized word.
The oil slick APPROACHES the coast of Texas.

Question #3:
Write the present perfect tense of the capitalized word.
The ash cloud from the volcano DRIFTS toward the island.

Question #4:
Write the future perfect tense of the capitalized word.
The Hardy Boys SOLVED the mystery

Question #5:
Write the present perfect tense of the capitalized word.
Sandy PLAYS the tuba in the marching band.

Question #6:
Write the future perfect tense of the capitalized word.
Janie RECORDS her favorite songs.

Question #7:
Write the present perfect tense of the capitalized word.
Peter Piper PICKS a peck of pickled peppers.

Question #8:
Write the past perfect tense of the capitalized word.
John SAVED them from being embarrassed.

Question #9:
Write the future perfect tense of the capitalized word.
We FINISH our novel on Friday.

Question #10:
Write the present perfect tense of the capitalized word.
He SERVED as president of the group for two years.

Question #11:
Choose the correct tense of the capitalized word(s).
Some people WILL HAVE WASTED their time.
   A.   future perfect
   B.   past perfect
   C.   present perfect

Question #12:
Choose the correct tense of the capitalized word(s).
In her dream, Emily HAD DANCED to a song that she loved.
   A.   present perfect
   B.   past perfect
   C.   future perfect

Question #13:
Choose the correct tense of the capitalized word(s).
Superman HAS JUMPED over buildings in a single bound.
   A.   past perfect
   B.   present perfect
   C.   future perfect

Question #14:
Choose the correct tense of the capitalized word(s).
The runner's legs HAD CRAMPED during the race.
   A.   past perfect
   B.   present perfect
   C.   future perfect

Question #15:
Choose the correct tense of the capitalized word(s).
Mr. Jones's beagle HAS CHASED cars since he was a puppy.
   A.   past perfect
   B.   future perfect
   C.   present perfect

Question #16:
Choose the correct tense of the capitalized word(s).
Thousands of people WILL HAVE JAMMED the stadium for the play-off.
   A.   present perfect
   B.   past perfect
   C.   future perfect

Question #17:
Which sentence is written using past perfect tense?
   A.   The dwarves arrived after Snow White has tasted the poisoned apple.
   B.   The dwarves arrived after Snow White will have tasted the poisoned apple.
   C.   The dwarves arrived after Snow White had tasted the poisoned apple.

VERB ROUNDUP

Identify the correct answer to each question

Question #18:
Which sentence is written using future perfect tense?
- A. By the time he finishes, I will have heard that lecture four times this
- B. By the time he finishes, I had heard that lecture four times this week.
- C. By the time he finishes, I have heard that lecture four times this week.

Question #19:
Which sentence is written using present perfect tense?
- A. She has lived there all her life.
- B. She will have lived there all her life.
- C. She had lived there all her life.

Question #20:
Which sentence is written using present perfect?
- A. The traffic jam has backed up the cars for two miles.
- B. The traffic jam will have backed up the cars for two miles.
- C. The traffic jam had backed up the cars for two miles.

Question #21:
Which sentence is written using future perfect tense?
- A. It may take all week, but by Friday he has completed the project.
- B. It may take all week, but by Friday he will have completed the project.
- C. It may take all week, but by Friday he had completed the project.

Question #22:
What is the tense of the verb in this sentence?
He has practiced that dive all summer.
- A. future perfect
- B. past perfect
- C. present perfect

Question #23:
What is the tense of the verb in this sentence?
Until now, he has only played his song for his parents.
- A. present perfect
- B. past perfect
- C. future perfect

Question #24:
What is the tense of the verb in this sentence?
Sam's success had paved the way for other hard-working students.
- A. future perfect
- B. present perfect
- C. past perfect

Question #25:
What is the tense of the verb in this sentence?
The clouds had covered the sun that day.
- A. present perfect
- B. past perfect
- C. future perfect

Answer Key
Begins Here

PAGE 5 ANSWERS
ALGEBRAIC EXPRESSIONS

1) 9 less than 4 times z
$$4z - 9$$

2) 8 is subtracted from n
$$n-8$$

3) 6 minus h
$$6-h$$

4) 4 times the sum of 9 and k
$$4(9+k)$$

5) k minus 2
$$k-2$$

6) 8 times the sum of p and 5
$$8(p+5)$$

7) Two-fifths of the sum of w and 7 minus the product of 6 and g
$$\frac{2}{5}(w+7) - 6g$$

8) Subtract two-thirds from 8 times q
$$8q - \frac{2}{3}$$

9) Four-fifths of the sum of w and 9 plus the product of 8 and x
$$\frac{4}{5}(w+9) + 8x$$

10) Sum of d and 3
$$d+3$$

PAGE 6 ANSWERS
ALGEBRAIC EXPRESSIONS

1) Add one-fourth to 9 times x

$$9x + \frac{1}{4}$$

2) Subtract three-fourths from 6 times k

$$6k - \frac{3}{4}$$

3) z squared plus the product of 9 and d plus 8

$$z^2 + 9d + 8$$

4) s is added to 2

$$s+2$$

5) Three-fifths of the sum of n and 6

$$\frac{3}{5}(n+6)$$

6) Take away 3 from 9 times c

$$9c - 3$$

7) 4 is added to h

$$4+h$$

8) 9 less than h

$$h-9$$

9) Take away 7 from r

$$r-7$$

10) 7 divided by n

$$7/n$$

PAGE 7 ANSWERS
GEOGRAPHY & MAPS

1. absolute location
2. latitude
3. isthmus
4. plateau
5. equator
6. prime meridian
7. monsoon
8. mouth of river
9. La Niña
10. delta
11. El Niño
12. relative location
13. longitude

PAGE 8 ANSWERS
GEOGRAPHY & MAPS

1. physical feature map
2. economic map
3. climate zone map
4. steppe
5. Tropic of Capricorn
6. archipelago
7. tundra
8. Tropic of Cancer
9. glacier
10. fjord
11. population density map
12. vegetation map
13. peninsula
14. gulf

PAGE 9 ANSWERS
SPELLING QUIZ

1. C
2. C
3. D
4. C
5. D

6. D
7. D
8. B
9. C
10. A

11. C
12. A
13. D
14. D
15. B

PAGE 10 ANSWERS
SPELLING QUIZ

1. D
2. C
3. D
4. B
5. B

6. C
7. B
8. B
9. B
10. B

11. A
12. D
13. B
14. A
15. C

PAGE 11 ANSWERS
SURFACE AREA & VOLUME

1)

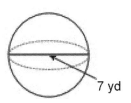

7 yd

Surface Area: 153.94 yd^2

Volume: 179.59 yd^3

2)

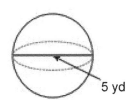

5 yd

Surface Area: 78.54 yd^2

Volume: 65.45 yd^3

3)

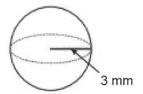

3 mm

Surface Area: 113.10 mm^2

Volume: 113.10 mm^3

4)

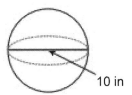

10 in

Surface Area: 314.16 in^2

Volume: 523.60 in^3

5)

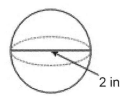

2 in

Surface Area: 12.57 in^2

Volume: 4.19 in^3

6)

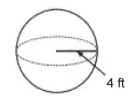

4 ft

Surface Area: 201.06 ft^2

Volume: 268.08 ft^3

7)

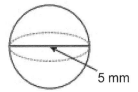

5 mm

Surface Area: 78.54 mm^2

Volume: 65.45 mm^3

8)

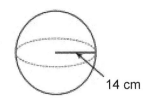

14 cm

Surface Area: 2463.01 cm^2

Volume: 11494.04 cm^3

9)

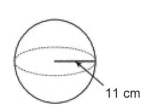

11 cm

Surface Area: 1520.53 cm^2

Volume: 5575.28 cm^3

PAGE 12 ANSWERS
SURFACE AREA & VOLUME

1)

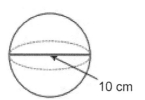

10 cm

Surface Area: 314.16 cm^2

Volume: 523.60 cm^3

2)

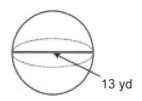

13 yd

Surface Area: 530.93 yd^2

Volume: 1150.35 yd^3

3)

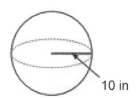

10 in

Surface Area: 1256.64 in^2

Volume: 4188.79 in^3

4)

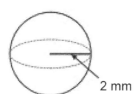

2 mm

Surface Area: 50.27 mm^2

Volume: 33.51 mm^3

5)

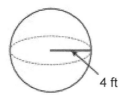

4 ft

Surface Area: 201.06 ft^2

Volume: 268.08 ft^3

6)

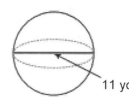

11 yd

Surface Area: 380.13 yd^2

Volume: 696.91 yd^3

7)

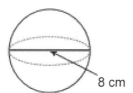

8 cm

Surface Area: 201.06 cm^2

Volume: 268.08 cm^3

8)

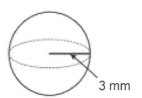

3 mm

Surface Area: 113.10 mm^2

Volume: 113.10 mm^3

9)

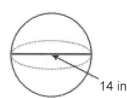

14 in

Surface Area: 615.75 in^2

Volume: 1436.76 in^3

PAGE 13 ANSWERS
HISTORY WORD SEARCH

adaptation	anthropologist	archaeologist	domestication
hunter gatherer	Neolithic	Paleolithic	paleontologist
hominids	agriculture	bipedal	Homo habilis
Homo erectus	Homo sapiens	Australopithecus	Neanderthal
primate	Stone Age	Mesolithic	prehistoric

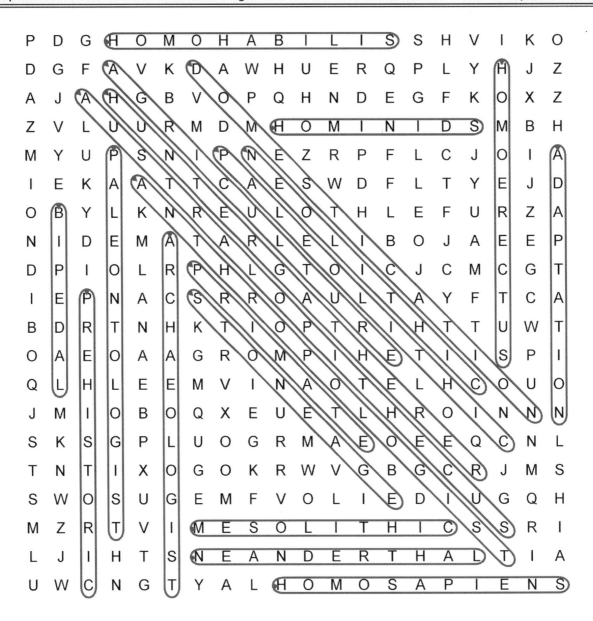

PAGE 14 ANSWERS
VOCABULARY FILL-INS

abandon	arrogant	coherent	cosmetic
gavel	lenient	pending	tolerance
polarize	immense		

1) Despite his kind persona, the movie star was incredibly _____ in real life, believing himself to be better than other people because of his wealth and status.

2) An excited David hit the dance floor immediately, proceeding to do the robot with total _____.

3) The defendant's reply caused an uproar in the courtroom, requiring the judge to bang his _____ and demand "ORDER!" for a solid minute.

4) Jason knew his controversial opinion that pineapple should be mandatory on all pizzas would _____ the class.

5) As it turned out, Kate's school was pretty _____ about enforcing the dress code, and she made it through the entire day without being asked to remove her clown wig.

6) Thankfully, the damage to my car was purely _____ and didn't affect its functionality.

7) My grandpa eats ghost peppers every day, so his _____ for spicy foods is off the charts!

8) I figured Jacob must still be half-asleep, since his strange ramblings weren't the least bit _____.

9) With the order status stuck on _____, Beto couldn't be certain that his pre-order was actually secured.

10) The mansion was an _____ beast, featuring several helicopter pads and a designated room just for eating cake.

1. __arrogant__   6. __cosmetic__

2. __abandon__   7. __tolerance__

3. __gavel__   8. __coherent__

4. __polarize__   9. __pending__

5. __lenient__   10. __immense__

PAGE 15-16 ANSWERS
WORLD HISTORY

1. D	1. A
2. A	2. D
3. A	3. D
4. C	4. B
5. C	5. C
6. C	6. D

PAGE 17-18 ANSWERS
WORLD HISTORY

1. A	1. C
2. D	2. B
3. D	3. A
4. C	
5. B	
6. D	

PAGE 19 ANSWERS
SYNONYMS CROSSWORD

loquacious	gargantuan	diminutive	redundant
dilemma	surmise	essential	courage
winsome	pallid	predictable	discourteous
ludicrous	frigid	innocuous	tranquil
trifling	remiss	nebulous	revolting

Across →
4. hazy
6. repetitive
8. guess
10. peaceful
12. huge
14. disgusting
17. problem
18. ridiculous
19. small
20. charming

Down ↓
1. harmless
2. expected
3. bravery
5. necessary
7. unimportant
9. impolite
11. cold
13. talkative
15. negligent
16. pale

PAGE 20 ANSWERS
SYNONYMS CROSSWORD

vague	flawless	congenial	compulsory
svelte	terminate	melancholy	expedite
callous	triumph	eccentric	sensitive
ebullient	uniform	disparate	hapless
antagonize	profuse	integrity	futile

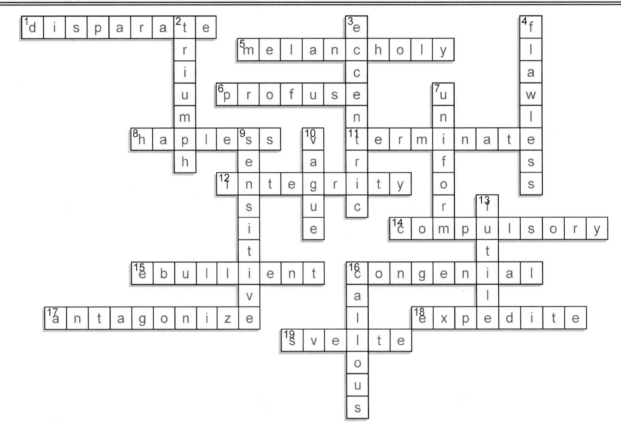

Across →

1. different
5. sadness
6. abundant
8. unfortunate
11. end
12. honesty
14. required
15. joyful
16. friendly
17. provoke
18. hurry
19. thin

Down ↓

2. succeed
3. unusual
4. perfect
7. alike
9. touchy
10. unclear
13. pointless
16. hardened

PAGE 21 ANSWERS
IDENTIFY SOLID FIGURES

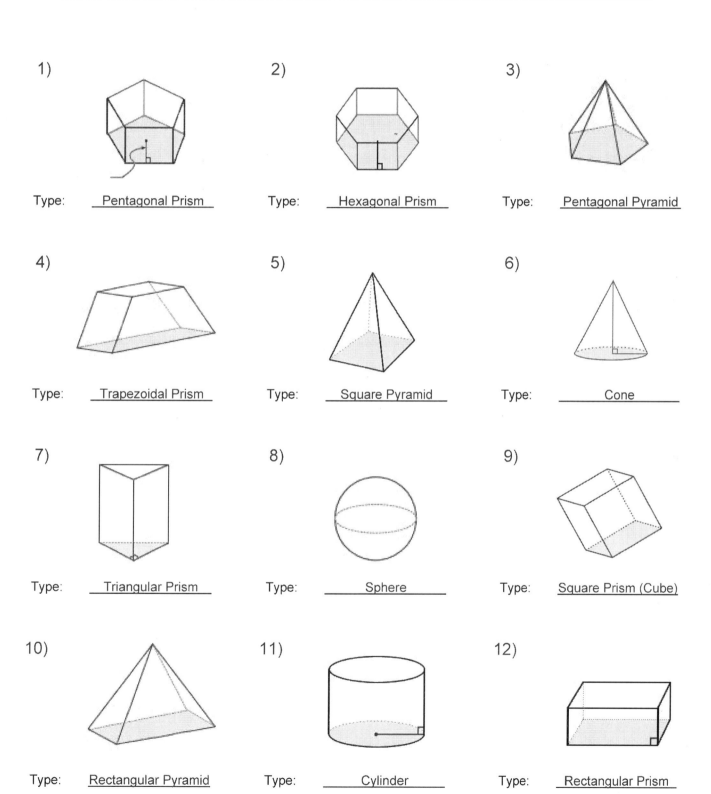

1)

Type: __Pentagonal Prism__

2)

Type: __Hexagonal Prism__

3)

Type: __Pentagonal Pyramid__

4)

Type: __Trapezoidal Prism__

5)

Type: __Square Pyramid__

6)

Type: __Cone__

7)

Type: __Triangular Prism__

8)

Type: __Sphere__

9)

Type: __Square Prism (Cube)__

10)

Type: __Rectangular Pyramid__

11)

Type: __Cylinder__

12)

Type: __Rectangular Prism__

PAGE 22 ANSWERS
IDENTIFY SOLID FIGURES

1)

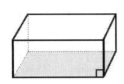

Type: Rectangular Prism

2)

Type: Pentagonal Pyramid

3)

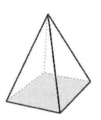

Type: Square Pyramid

4)

Type: Pentagonal Prism

5)

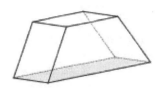

Type: Trapezoidal Prism

6)

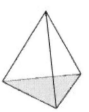

Type: Triangular Pyramid

7)

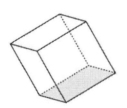

Type: Square Prism (Cube)

8)

Type: Cone

9)

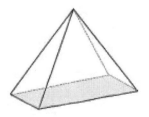

Type: Rectangular Pyramid

10)

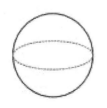

Type: Sphere

11)

Type: Hexagonal Prism

12)

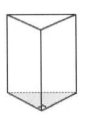

Type: Triangular Prism

PAGE 23 ANSWERS
PROPERTIES OF WAVES

1. amplitude
2. transverse waves
3. gamma waves
4. wavelength
5. x-ray
6. frequency
7. crest
8. trough
9. electromagnetic spectrum
10. mechanical waves
11. photon
12. radio waves
13. visible light
14. infrared waves
15. ultraviolet

PAGE 24 ANSWERS
PROPERTIES OF WAVES

1. radio waves
2. Michael Faraday
3. infrared
4. x-ray
5. Heinrich Hertz
6. Hans Christian Ørsted
7. ultraviolet waves
8. gamma rays
9. James Clerk Maxwell
10. visible light waves
11. radiation
12. energy
13. microwaves

PAGE 25-28 ANSWERS
HEALTH SMARTS

1: B
2: C
3: A
4: B
5: C

6: C
7: D
8: D
9: D
10: C

11: A
12: A
13: B
14: B
15: C

16: C
17: B
18: C
19: B
20: D

21: C
22: D
23: B
24: C
25: B

PAGE 29 ANSWERS
HEALTH SMARTS

1) (True / False) Drinking alcohol is an effective, long-lasting method for coping with your problems.

2) (True / False) Excessive alcohol consumption can increase your risk of developing certain cancers.

3) (True / False) Vaping is a perfectly healthy alternative to smoking tobacco, since it never has any negative consequences.

4) (True / False) If you simply exercise strong willpower when using drugs, then you won't face any problems with substance abuse.

5) (True / False) Cigarette smoking is the #1 cause of preventable deaths in the United States.

6) (True / False) Chewing tobacco is actually a very safe habit because it doesn't damage your lungs.

7) (True / False) As long as you're not blackout drunk, it's still pretty safe to drive a motor vehicle.

8) (True / False) Although vaping nicotine is less harmful overall than smoking cigarettes, it is still highly addictive.

9) (True / False) Prescription drugs are safe and nothing to worry about, since they're prescribed legally by doctors every single day.

10) (True / False) Cigarette smoke contains a large number of carcinogens -- i.e. substances that can cause cancer in living tissues.

1. ___false___
2. ___true___
3. ___false___
4. ___false___
5. ___true___

6. ___false___
7. ___false___
8. ___true___
9. ___false___
10. ___true___

PAGE 30 ANSWERS
WAVES WORD SEARCH

energy	electromagnetic	frequency	amplitude
transverse	longitudinal	wavelength	interference
constructive	destructive	crest	trough
medium	reflection	refraction	diffraction
velocity	radiation	photon	

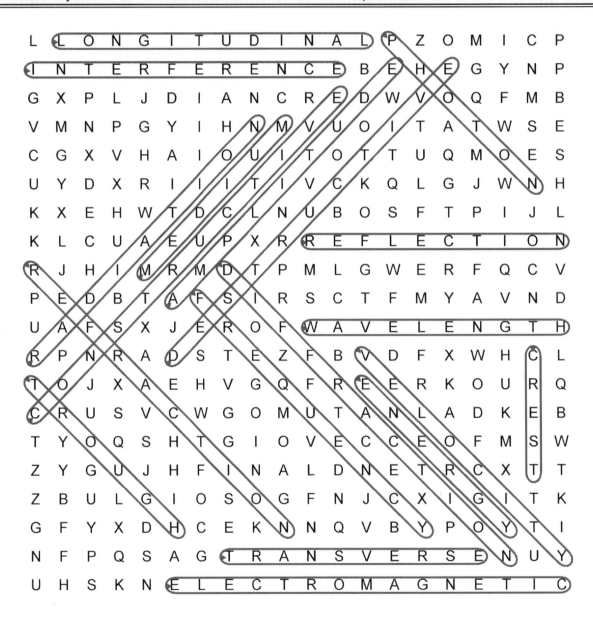

PAGE 31 ANSWERS
WORLD HISTORY FILL-INS

Marshall Plan	United Nations	Cold War	communism
Korean War	38th parallel	SEATO	Cuban Missile Crisis
NATO	Joseph McCarthy	Khrushchev	

1) The _____ started because communist North Koreans invaded South Korea.

2) The _____ was a long, bitter struggle between the United States and the Soviet Union.

3) After Stalin's death, _____ took control, acting as First Secretary of the Soviet Union's Communist Party.

4) During the 1950's, senator _____ became convinced that communists were trying to take over the U.S. government.

5) The _____ was formed as an organization that would promote global cooperation.

6) The _____ was set up to help Europe recover from WWII.

7) Soviets believed in _____, whereas the Americans believed in democracy.

8) United States troops helped guard the _____ (border zone) between North Korea and South Korea after the Korean War.

9) In 1949, the United States entered a military alliance known as _____.

10) The _____ occurred because Soviets were setting up nuclear missiles in Cuba.

11) _____ was established to protect Southeast Asian countries against the spread of communism.

1. **Korean War**
2. **Cold War**
3. **Khrushchev**
4. **Joseph McCarthy**
5. **United Nations**
6. **Marshall Plan**
7. **communism**
8. **38th parallel**
9. **NATO**
10. **Cuban Missile Crisis**
11. **SEATO**

PAGE 32 ANSWERS
1-STEP EQUATIONS

1) $c + \frac{5}{8} = 7$

$c = 6.38$

2) $\frac{1}{3} = \frac{2}{5} + n$

$n = -0.07$

3) $f + 22\frac{2}{9} = 19$

$f = -3.22$

4) $d + 12 = -11\frac{7}{9}$

$d = -23.78$

5) $26\frac{1}{9} + k = 24$

$k = -2.11$

6) $\frac{2}{9}r = 7$

$r = 31.50$

7) $22\frac{5}{8} = -4\frac{6}{7} + x$

$x = 27.48$

8) $19\frac{8}{9} = 2\frac{5}{7}a$

$a = 7.33$

9) $\frac{2}{9} = v - \frac{7}{8}$

$v = 1.10$

10) $-14\frac{1}{8}b = 25\frac{5}{8}$

$b = -1.81$

PAGE 33 ANSWERS
1-STEP EQUATIONS

1) $29\frac{4}{7} = -12\frac{7}{8} + k$

    k = 42.45

6) $\frac{4}{7}c = 7$

    c = 12.25

2) $v - 24\frac{4}{9} = 26$

    v = 50.44

7) $\frac{2}{3} = a + \frac{1}{5}$

    a = 0.47

3) $22\frac{3}{4} = -3\frac{1}{3}b$

    b = -6.82

8) $\frac{4}{5} + f = 5$

    f = 4.20

4) $\frac{2}{3} = -\frac{1}{9} + h$

    h = 0.78

9) $r - 12 = -20\frac{6}{7}$

    r = -8.86

5) $4\frac{2}{5} + s = -24\frac{1}{9}$

    s = -28.51

10) $y - \frac{2}{5} = 18$

    y = 18.40

PAGE 34 ANSWERS
VOCAB MATCH GAME

1. astute
2. ecstasy
3. germinate
4. verbatim
5. admirable

6. brazen
7. capricious
8. bereavement
9. enunciate
10. aquatic

11. postpone
12. decent
13. commodities
14. revive
15. unlucky

PAGE 35 ANSWERS
VOCAB MATCH GAME

1. charitable
2. voluntary
3. obvious
4. overbearing
5. ambiguous

6. valor
7. descendant
8. ancestor
9. clarify
10. announce

11. vindicate
12. entrust
13. impulsive
14. frugal
15. terrestrial

PAGE 36-37 ANSWERS
WEATHER PATTERNS

1. The layer of gases that surrounds Earth is called the <u>atmosphere</u>
2. The two most abundant gases in the atmosphere are <u>nitrogen and oxygen</u>
3. Water vapor is water in the form of a <u>gas</u>
4. Earth's atmosphere is important to living things because it provides <u>all the gases that living things need to survive</u>
5. Air has pressure because air has <u>mass</u>
6. Instruments used to measure air pressure are called <u>barometers</u>
7. The air pressure acting on the roof of your house comes from <u>all the air above your roof</u>
8. As you rise upwards in the atmosphere, air pressure <u>decreases</u>
9. Clouds form when water vapor in the air becomes <u>liquid water or ice crystals</u>
10. When climbing a high mountain, you get out of breath easily because <u>there is less oxygen in each cubic meter of air</u>
11. The layer of our atmosphere in which weather occurs is the <u>troposphere</u>
12. The ozone layer protects living things on Earth from <u>ultraviolet radiation</u>
13. Most air pollution comes from burning <u>fossil fuels</u>
14. Most of Earth's incoming ultraviolet radiation is absorbed by <u>ozone</u>
15. The greenhouse effect is <u>the process by which gases hold heat in the atmosphere</u>
16. The freezing point of pure water on the Celsius scale is <u>0°C</u>
17. Heat from the sun reaches you by <u>radiation</u>
18. Convection takes place because cold air is more <u>dense than warm air</u>
19. Winds are caused by differences in <u>air pressure</u>
20. Cool air tends to be more dense and flow <u>under warm air.</u>
21. Wind speed is measured by a(n) <u>anemometer</u>
22. Land breezes occur because land <u>cools off faster than water</u>
23. Global winds generally blow <u>from specific directions over long distances</u>
24. Earth's rotation makes global winds curve. This is called the <u>Coriolis effect</u>
25. The doldrums are characterized by <u>weak winds</u>
26. Relative humidity can be measured with a(an) <u>psychrometer</u>
27. Two conditions are required for cloud formation: cooling of the air and <u>the presence of particles in the air</u>
28. Large clouds that often produce thunderstorms are called <u>cumulonimbus clouds</u>
29. Very high feathery clouds are called <u>cirrus clouds</u>
30. Layered clouds that often cover much of the sky and are a dull gray color are called <u>stratus clouds</u>
31. Any form of water that falls from clouds is called <u>precipitation</u>
32. Cold, dry air affecting the northern United States in winter often comes from <u>continental polar air masses</u>
33. When a rapidly moving cold air mass overtakes a slow-moving warm air mass, the result is a(n) <u>cold front</u>
34. When a warm air mass and a cold air mass meet and neither can move the other, the result is a(n) <u>stationary front</u>
35. A funnel-shaped cloud that touches Earth's surface is called a <u>tornado</u>
36. One of the best places to seek protection during a tornado is <u>in the basement of a well-built building</u>
37. Weather forecasting has improved recently in part because of improved <u>data gathering and computer technology</u>
38. Scientists who study weather and try to predict it are called <u>meteorologists</u>
39. Isobars are lines on a map joining places that have the same <u>air pressure</u>
40. On weather maps, a line with half circles indicates a <u>warm front</u>
41. What kind of weather would a continental tropical air mass that formed over northern Mexico bring to the southwestern United States? <u>Hot and dry</u>
42. Tornado Alley includes the states of <u>Texas, Oklahoma, Kansas, Nebraska, Missouri, Iowa and South Dakota</u>
43. Hurricanes typically form over warm <u>ocean water</u>
44. The eye of a hurricane is <u>calm</u>
45. Which source of weather data would enable a meteorologist to follow the path of an approaching thunderstorm? <u>Radar</u>
46. The prevailing westerlies, the major wind belts over the continental United States, generally push air masses from <u>west to east</u>
47. One example of a safe place to be during a thunderstorm is crouching in <u>a low area</u>
48. If people are asked to evacuate during a hurricane watch, they are being asked to <u>leave the area temporarily</u>
49. The cycle of heating, rising, cooling, and sinking is called a <u>convection current</u>
50. What is the most abundant gas in air? <u>Nitrogen</u>

Use the diagram to answer each question

Local Winds

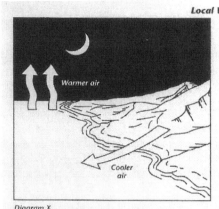

Diagram X

Diagram Y

51. In diagram X, from which way does the wind blow? Land or sea? <u>Land</u>

52. In diagram Y, from which way does the wind blow? Land or sea? <u>Sea</u>

53. Which diagram shows the formation of a sea breeze? <u>Diagram Y</u>

54. Which diagram shows the formation of a land breeze? <u>Diagram X</u>

55. In diagram X, which cools more quickly, the land or water? <u>Land</u>

Use the diagram to answer each question

Weather Map

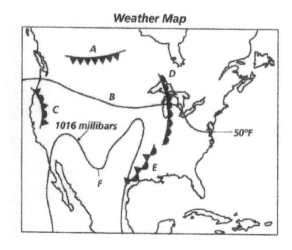

56. What does A represent? In what direction is it moving? <u>Cold front moving south</u>

57. What is B called? <u>Isotherm</u>

58. What does D represent? In what direction is it moving? <u>Warm front moving east</u>

59. What does E represent? <u>Stationary front</u>

60. What does F connect? <u>Points of equal air pressure</u>

PAGE 39-40 ANSWERS
VERBS FOR THE WIN

1. design
2. approve
3. level
4. require
5. are

6. unroll
7. love
8. B -abandon
9. B -achieve
10. B -jiggle

11. A -examine
12. B -begin
13. is
14. was
15. looks

16. became
17. are
18. feel
19. seems
20. was

21. is
22. appears
23. begins
24. chooses
25. place

PAGE 41 ANSWERS
PRISMS & CYLINDERS

1)

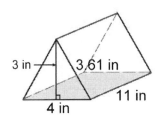

3 in   3.61 in

11 in

4 in

Surface Area: _135.42 in²_

2)

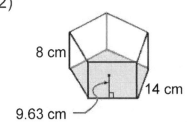

8 cm

14 cm

9.63 cm

Surface Area: _1234.10 cm²_

3)

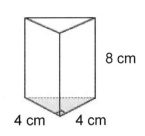

8 cm

4 cm   4 cm

Surface Area: _125.25 cm²_

4)

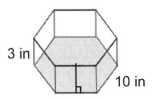

3 in

10 in

Surface Area: _699.62 in²_

5)

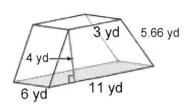

3 yd   5.66 yd

4 yd

6 yd   11 yd

Surface Area: _207.92 yd²_

6)

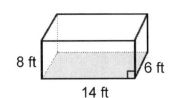

8 ft

6 ft

14 ft

Surface Area: _488.00 ft²_

7)

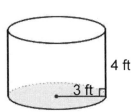

4 ft

3 ft

Surface Area: _131.95 ft²_

8)

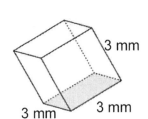

3 mm

3 mm

3 mm

Surface Area: _54.00 mm²_

9)

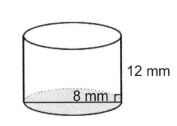

12 mm

8 mm

Surface Area: _402.12 mm²_

PAGE 42 ANSWERS
PRISMS & CYLINDERS

1)

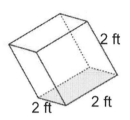

2 ft
2 ft   2 ft
2 ft

Surface Area: __24.00 ft²__

2)

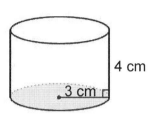

4 cm
3 cm

Surface Area: __131.95 cm²__

3)

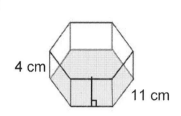

4 cm
11 cm

Surface Area: __892.73 cm²__

4)

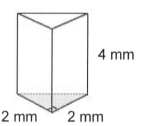

4 mm
2 mm   2 mm

Surface Area: __31.31 mm²__

5)

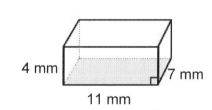

4 mm
7 mm
11 mm

Surface Area: __298.00 mm²__

6)

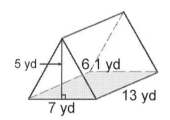

5 yd   6.1 yd
13 yd
7 yd

Surface Area: __284.60 yd²__

7)

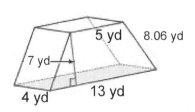

5 yd   8.06 yd
7 yd
4 yd   13 yd

Surface Area: __262.48 yd²__

8)

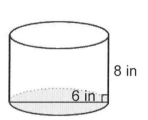

8 in
6 in

Surface Area: __207.35 in²__

9)

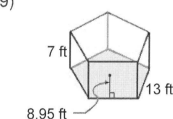

7 ft
13 ft
8.95 ft

Surface Area: __1036.75 ft²__

PAGE 43 ANSWERS
TRUE OR FALSE: SPACE

1. true
2. true
3. true
4. true
5. true

6. false
7. true
8. false
9. true
10. false

PAGE 44 ANSWERS
TRUE OR FALSE: SPACE

1. true
2. true
3. false
4. true
5. true

6. true
7. true
8. false
9. false
10. true

PAGE 45 ANSWERS
RELIGIONS CROSSWORD

Brahmanism	Buddhism	Christianity	Confucianism
Hinduism	Daoism	religion	Torah
Vedas	monotheism	synagogue	Judaism
Exodus	karma		

Across →

2. the first five books of the Jewish Bible
5. a place of Jewish worship
6. a set of spiritual beliefs, values and practices
8. a major world religion that was founded by the Hebrews
10. an ancient Indian religion in which the Brahmins (priests and religious scholars) are the dominant class
11. a collection of Hindu sacred writings
13. India's first major religion; the third largest religion after Christianity and Islam
14. the belief that there is only one God

Down ↓

1. a Chinese philosophy that emphasizes living in harmony with nature
3. the religion based on the life and teachings of Jesus Christ
4. a Chinese philosophy that emphasizes proper behavior
7. the escape of the Hebrews from Egyptian slavery
9. in Hinduism, the belief that how a person lives will affect their next life
12. a religion of India begun by Prince Siddhartha, or the Buddha

PAGE 46 ANSWERS
CIVILIZATION CROSSWORD

aqueduct	civilization	emperor	empire
culture	imperial	republic	irrigation
migration	politics	merchant	settlement

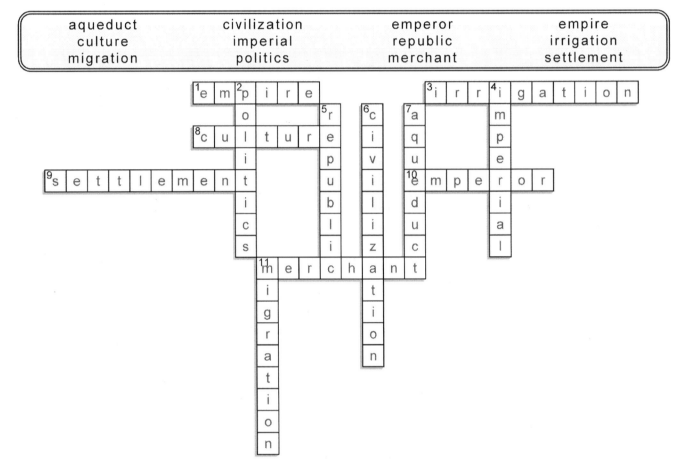

Across →

1. a large territory in which several groups of people are ruled by a single leader or government
3. a means of supplying land with water
8. a characteristic of civilization that includes the beliefs and behaviors of a society or group of people
9. a small community or village
10. the leader of an empire
11. a person who makes money by selling goods

Down ↓

2. having to do with government
4. having to do with an empire
5. a form of government with elected leaders
6. a culture marked by developments in arts, sciences, government and social structure
7. a pipe or channel that brings water from distant places
11. moving from one geographic region to another

PAGE 47 ANSWERS
NATURAL DISASTERS

1. What are three things needed to triangulate the epicenter of an earthquake?
    a. *A minimum of three seismograph stations*
    b. *Arrival of P Waves*
    c. *Arrival of S Waves*

2. Name three things that can cause tsunamis.
    a. *Undersea earthquakes*
    b. *Landslides*
    c. *Volcanic eruptions*

3. What happens as tsunamis move toward shore?

    They increase in height

4. What do scientists record to find the epicenter of an earthquake?

    Record arrival of P and S waves

5. What is the difference between the epicenter and the focus of an earthquake?

    The epicenter is the point on Earth's surface directly above the focus.

6. Why do earthquakes usually occur at plate boundaries?

    Rock environments near tectonic plate boundaries experience great stress.

7. What should you do if inside during an earthquake?

    Stay away from windows.

8. What should you do if inside a car during an earthquake?

    Stop the car in a safe place.

9. Describe intensity XII on the Mercalli Scale.

    Causes total destruction

10. How does the ground move under the influence of Rayleigh waves?

    In an elliptical, rolling motion

PAGE 48 ANSWERS
NATURAL DISASTERS

11. Name three things that signal a volcanic eruption.

    A change in earthquake activity

    Bulging volcano surface

    A change in the amount and composition of volcanic gases

12. What is another name for composite volcanoes?

    stratovolcanoes

13. What happens at a convergent boundary when an island arc forms?

    Oceanic lithosphere subducts beneath oceanic lithosphere.

14. Which scale most accurately measures a large magnitude earthquake?

    Moment Magnitude Scale

15. What happens to buildings during an earthquake?

    It may sway or collapse.

16. Which magnitude scales express measurements numerically?

    Both the Richter and the Moment Magnitude Scales

17. What is the difference between the Richter and Mercalli Scales?

    The Richter Scale measures magnitude; The Mercalli Scale measures intensity.

18. Which type of volcano is made up of pyroclastic material?

    Cinder Cone

19. Name three ways to classify a volcanic eruption.

    Lava flows, Quiet, Explosive

20. Compare the chemical compositions of mafic and felsic magma.

    Mafic magma is rich in magnesium and iron; felsic magma is rich in feldspar and silica

21. How does the chemical composition of magma affect the explosivity of a volcanic eruption?

    Low-viscosity magma causes quiet eruptions; high-viscosity magma causes explosive eruptions

PAGE 49 ANSWERS
GRAPHING INEQUALITIES

1) $s \leq 9$
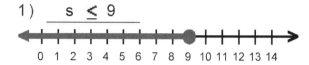

2) $s \leq -0.5$

3) $3 \leq r$

4) $-b > -1$ or $b < 1$
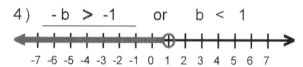

5) $3 > d$
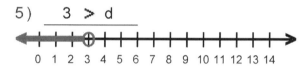

6) $5 \geq w$
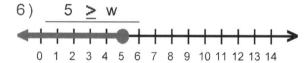

7) $-2.5 \leq -f$ or $2.5 \geq f$

8) $-j > -1$ or $j < 1$
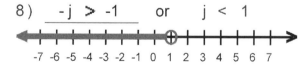

9) $-0.5 \geq -z$ or $0.5 \leq z$
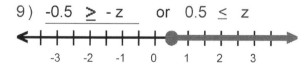

10) $13 < a$
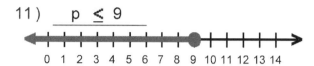

11) $p \leq 9$

12) $-z > -4$ or $z < 4$
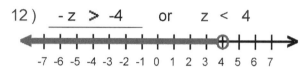

13) $-1.5 \geq -v$ or $1.5 \leq v$
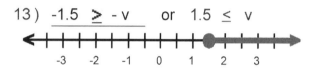

14) $2.5 \geq a$
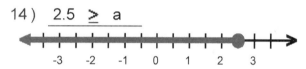

15) $10 < k$
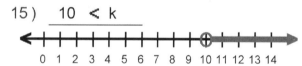

16) $-f > 0.5$ or $f < -0.5$
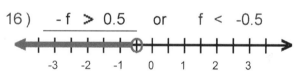

17) $v \geq -1$
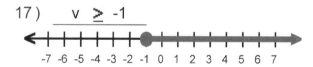

18) $2 < -g$ or $-2 > g$

19) $p < -3$
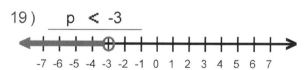

20) $-n < -2$ or $n > 2$
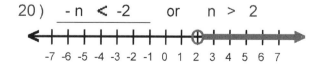

PAGE 50 ANSWERS
GRAPHING INEQUALITIES

1) $k > -1$

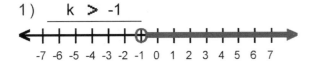

2) $8 < a$

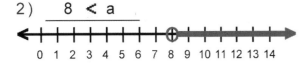

3) $-1.5 > w$

4) $13 \geq f$

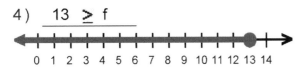

5) $4 > f$

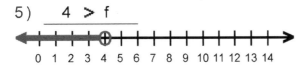

6) $12 \leq z$

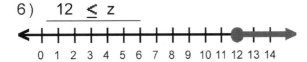

7) $h < -5$

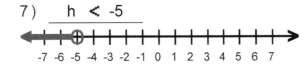

8) $c \leq 0.5$

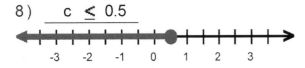

9) $y < -2$

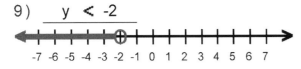

10) $g \leq 3$

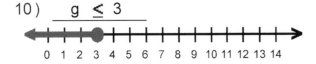

11) $-3 \geq w$

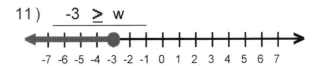

12) $3 \geq b$

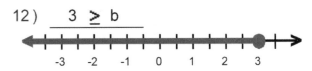

13) $y > -0.5$

14) $w \geq 4$

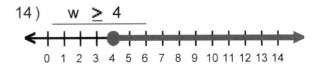

15) $4 < c$

16) $-1 > k$

17) $h < -2$

18) $z \geq -2.5$

19) $a \leq -1$

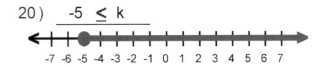

20) $-5 \leq k$

PAGE 51 ANSWERS
ADD/SUBTRACT INEQUALITIES

1) k ≥ -18

2) y < 11

3) w < -15

4) q ≥ 16

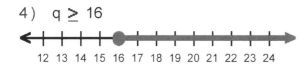

5) z > -17

6) g ≥ -4

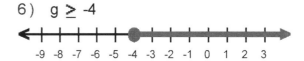

7) h ≤ -13

8) v < 1

9) a ≤ -10

10) b < 11

PAGE 52 ANSWERS
ADD/SUBTRACT INEQUALITIES

1) j ≥ -15

6) h > 13

2) x ≥ -18

7) v < -8

3) d ≤ 16

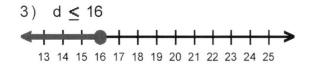

8) k ≥ -13

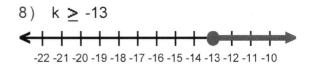

4) w > -11

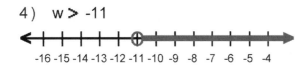

9) n ≥ 10

5) y > 9

10) s < -2

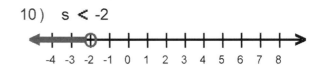

PAGE 53 ANSWERS
SUPER SPELLER QUIZ

1. C
2. D
3. D
4. A
5. B

6. A
7. C
8. D
9. B
10. D

11. B
12. B
13. C
14. A
15. A

PAGE 54 ANSWERS
SUPER SPELLER QUIZ

1. A
2. D
3. D
4. B
5. B

6. A
7. A
8. D
9. A
10. C

11. D
12. A
13. A
14. B
15. A

PAGE 55-56 ANSWERS
VERB MASTERY

1. A -approached
2. B -carried
3. B -attended
4. C -passed
5. A -appeared

6. A -will begin
7. A -was taking
8. A -are jumping
9. B -will be competing
10. A -has helped

11. A -will be
12. B -have been sitting
13. B -will ride
14. C -are watching
15. B -should swim

16. B -was not
17. B -cannot
18. A -would not
19. C -have not
20. B -She will

21. A -crushed
22. B -ties
23. B -admires
24. A -saved
25. C -opens

124

PAGE 57 ANSWERS
CHEMISTRY MATCH GAME

1. physical change
2. chemical equation
3. precipitate
4. closed system
5. reactants

6. open system
7. exothermic reaction
8. chemical change
9. endothermic reaction
10. products

PAGE 58 ANSWERS
CHEMISTRY MATCH GAME

1. activation energy
2. inhibitor
3. catalyst
4. replacement
5. law of conservation of mass

6. coefficient
7. concentration
8. enzyme
9. synthesis
10. decomposition

PAGE 59 ANSWERS
VOLCANO WORD SEARCH

earthquakes	volcanoes	epicenter	magnitude
mid-ocean ridge	shadow zone	intensity	subduction zone
pyroclastic material	focus	magma	pillow lava
seismology	hot spot	elastic rebound	pahoehoe
caldera	convection		

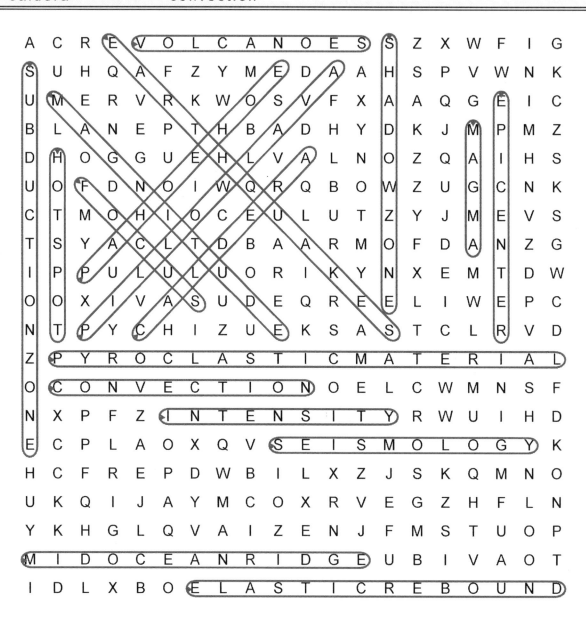

PAGE 60 ANSWERS
EQUIVALENT RATIOS

1) 3 : 8 = 6 :16 = 9 :24 = 12 :32 = 15 :40 = 18 :48

2) 1 : 2 = 2 : 4 = 3 : 6 = 4 : 8 = 5 :10 = 6 :12

3) 1 : 4 = 2 : 8 = 3 :12 = 4 :16 = 5 :20 = 6 :24

4) 1 :10 = 2 :20 = 3 :30 = 4 :40 = 5 :50 = 6 :60

5) 2 : 5 = 4 :10 = 6 :15 = 8 :20 = 10 :25 = 12 :30

6) 2 : 9 = 4 :18 = 6 :27 = 8 :36 = 10 :45 = 12 :54

7) 1 : 3 = 2 : 6 = 3 : 9 = 4 :12 = 5 :15 = 6 :18

8) 2 : 7 = 4 :14 = 6 :21 = 8 :28 = 10 :35 = 12 :42

9) 1 : 6 = 2 :12 = 3 :18 = 4 :24 = 5 :30 = 6 :36

10) 1 : 3 = 2 : 6 = 3 : 9 = 4 :12 = 5 :15 = 6 :18

PAGE 61 ANSWERS
EQUIVALENT RATIOS

1) 36 : 45 = 8 : 10 = 20 : 25 = 4 : 5 = 40 : 50 = 12 : 15

2) 9 : 36 = 2 : 8 = 5 : 20 = 1 : 4 = 10 : 40 = 3 : 12

3) 9 : 72 = 2 : 16 = 5 : 40 = 1 : 8 = 10 : 80 = 3 : 24

4) 18 : 63 = 4 : 14 = 10 : 35 = 2 : 7 = 20 : 70 = 6 : 21

5) 18 : 45 = 4 : 10 = 10 : 25 = 2 : 5 = 20 : 50 = 6 : 15

6) 18 : 27 = 4 : 6 = 10 : 15 = 2 : 3 = 20 : 30 = 6 : 9

7) 36 : 81 = 8 : 18 = 20 : 45 = 4 : 9 = 40 : 90 = 12 : 27

8) 9 : 27 = 2 : 6 = 5 : 15 = 1 : 3 = 10 : 30 = 3 : 9

9) 9 : 18 = 2 : 4 = 5 : 10 = 1 : 2 = 10 : 20 = 3 : 6

10) 45 : 54 = 10 : 12 = 25 : 30 = 5 : 6 = 50 : 60 = 15 : 18

PAGE 62-63 ANSWERS
GEOLOGY & EARTH SCIENCE

Compare and contrast the Earth's crust, mantle, and core including temperature, density, and composition.

1. Describe the state of matter and composition of the mantle (for all 3 layers). Crust: solid rock, mostly granite and basalt; Mantle: Solid and liquid rock; Core: outer core is liquid iron and nickel, inner is solid iron and nickel
2. Which layer of earth is made up of tectonic plates? lithosphere
3. How do we know what the inside of the earth looks like and what it is made of? By recording and studying seismic waves
4. What happens to the earth's pressure the deeper you go into the earth? It increases
5. The Outer Core is responsible for making the earth's magnetic field.
6. The core is mostly made up of iron & nickel
7. Describe the difference between the core and the mantle in terms of temperature and density: the core has higher temperatures and density

Investigate the contribution of minerals to rock composition.

8. What are minerals made of? elements
9. What do all minerals have in common? inorganic, solid, naturally formed, crystal structure, unique make-up/composition
10. True or False: Minerals are or once were organic.
11. Define the following terms as they relate to minerals:
Streak: the color of the mineral in its powdered form
Luster: way the mineral reflects light (metallic, dull, glassy, etc)
Cleavage: tendency of a mineral to break in smooth pattern
Fracture: tendency of a mineral to break in a rough and jagged manner

Mineral	Hardness	Way it breaks	Luster	Streak	Color
Galena	2.5	cleavage	metallic	gray-black	silver, gray
Magnetite	6	fracture	metallic	black	black
Hematite	6	fracture	metallic-dull	red-brown	red-brown, silver, black

12. *Use the chart above to answer this question:* Susan wants to identify a dark, heavy mineral sample she found in the classroom collection. She notices there are three minerals in a chart in a reference book that might match her sample. Susan next observes that her sample mineral has flat, reflective surfaces that break into boxlike steps. She infers the mineral may be galena. If she is correct, one more test will verify her inference. Which property would to best for her to observe next? hardness

Classify rocks by their process of formation.

13. What is the difference between intrusive and extrusive? Intrusive is formed inside the earth by the cooling of magma; extrusive is formed outside the earth by the cooling of lava
14. How do each of the following rock types form?
Sedimentary: WEDCC (weathering, erosion, deposition, compaction, cementation)
Metamorphic: heat and /or pressure
Igneous: melting and cooling of magma/lava
15. Why do some igneous rocks have holes? Bubbles of air were trapped in the rock when it cooled
16. Tell about the traits that are unique to each type of rock:
Sedimentary: breaks easily/ crumbly, fossils, layers, pebbles are visible
Metamorphic: small crystals, bands
Igneous: smooth and glassy, gas bubble holes, large crystals

Explain the effects of physical processes (plate tectonics, erosion, deposition, volcanic eruption, gravity) on geological features including oceans (composition, currents, and tides).

17. Tectonic plates are found in which layer of earth? lithosphere
18. Why was Alfred Wegener's idea of continental drift not accepted? Could not explain "how" the plates moved
19. What is subduction? The process of the ocean floor sinking beneath another plate and back into the mantle

PAGE 64-65 ANSWERS
GEOLOGY & EARTH SCIENCE

20. Where can we see the results of plate movement? Plate boundaries and rift valleys

21. What is the MAIN reason that the continents look very different than they did 100 million years ago? The continents has drifted apart from one another on lithospheric plates due to convection currents in the mantle

22. Convection Currents cause the movement of earth's tectonic or lithospheric plates

23. What evidence supports the theory of continental drift? Fossil clues, rock/mountain clues, climate/glacier clues

24. What geographic force forms u-shaped valleys? glaciers

25. On a topographical map there are curved contour lines that make complete, concentric loops that get smaller and smaller. What is inside the smallest loop? A hill or mountain

26. A contour interval shows the change in elevations

(Use the picture to the right to answer the questions #27-29)

27. What is the elevation of the star? 160

28. Which letter represents a steep slope? B

29. What is the contour interval for this topographical map? 20

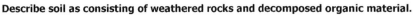

30. What force causes sediments to be moved from one area to another? Erosion (via water, ice or wind)

Describe soil as consisting of weathered rocks and decomposed organic material.

31. True or False Organic Matter is made of sand, silt, & clay, does not help plants grow, and is the only ingredient in soil

32. What is humus? Decomposed organic matter

33. Where does soil get its nutrients? When organic matter decays and turns into humus

34. Humus is found in which layer of soil? A horizon/ topsoil

35. What is leaching? When minerals are dissolved and carried from the A horizon to the B horizon

Students will describe various sources of energy, as well as their uses and conservation.

36. What is conservation? The process of using resources wisely; reduce, reuse, recycle

37. Define biomass the burning of organic matter, wood, or garbage used to generate energy

38. What is alternative energy? Name the different types of alternative energy. Alternative energy is another energy sources other than fossil fuels; Solar, Wind, Hydroelectric, Biomass, Nuclear, Geothermal

39. I am used mainly in the western US. My energy comes from the heat within the Earth. I can be used for home heating. Water that is piped down to me is turned into steam used to turn turbines and generate energy. What am I? geothermal

Identify renewable and nonrenewable resources.

40. Which of these items was made from a nonrenewable resource? Paper bag, motor oil, cotton shirt, wooden table

41. What is the difference between a renewable and a recyclable resource? Renewable can be replaced by nature in a short amount of time; recyclable is an item that is treated for reuse

42. How can having more people on earth impact our use of fossil fuels? The world's population is growing and more people are using natural resources faster than they can be replaced.

43. How are fossil fuels formed? From the remains of decayed plants and animals that have been buried millions of years ago

44. Natural gas, oil, and coal are all known as fossil fuels

PAGE 66 ANSWERS
COSMOS MATCH GAME

1. solar system
2. Mars
3. International Space Station
4. star
5. the Moon
6. astronaut
7. Earth
8. energy
9. the Sun
10. Mercury
11. Venus
12. lunar
13. research
14. Saturn
15. the universe
16. Milky Way
17. Neptune

PAGE 67 ANSWERS
COSMOS MATCH GAME

1. meteorite
2. space
3. meteor showers
4. technology
5. comet dust
6. Oort cloud
7. Titan
8. galaxy
9. satellite
10. asteroid
11. comet
12. astronomical unit
13. terrestrial planets
14. ellipses
15. moon phases
16. asteroid belt

PAGE 68 ANSWERS
PRISMS & PYRAMIDS

1)

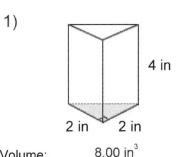

4 in

2 in   2 in

Volume: _____8.00 in³_____

2)

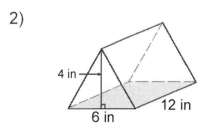

4 in

6 in   12 in

Volume: _____144.00 in³_____

3)

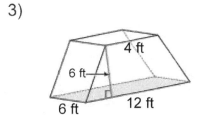

4 ft

6 ft

6 ft   12 ft

Volume: _____288.00 ft³_____

4)

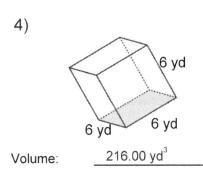

6 yd

6 yd   6 yd

Volume: _____216.00 yd³_____

5)

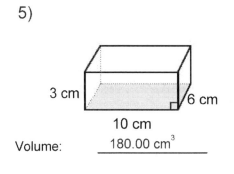

3 cm

6 cm

10 cm

Volume: _____180.00 cm³_____

6)

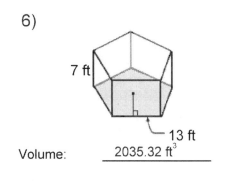

7 ft

13 ft

Volume: _____2035.32 ft³_____

7)

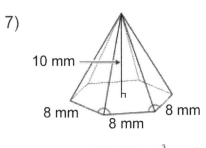

10 mm

8 mm   8 mm
8 mm

Volume: _____554.26 mm³_____

8)

10 mm

2 mm
2 mm

Volume: _____13.33 mm³_____

9)

10 yd

8 yd
8 yd   8 yd

Volume: _____367.04 yd³_____

PAGE 69 ANSWERS
PRISMS & PYRAMIDS

1)

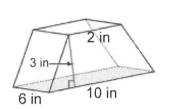

2 in

3 in

6 in   10 in

Volume: 108.00 in³

2)

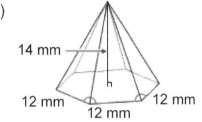

14 mm

12 mm   12 mm

12 mm

Volume: 1745.91 mm³

3)

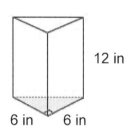

12 in

6 in   6 in

Volume: 216.00 in³

4)

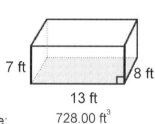

7 ft   8 ft

13 ft

Volume: 728.00 ft³

5)

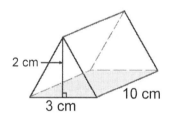

2 cm

3 cm   10 cm

Volume: 30.00 cm³

6)

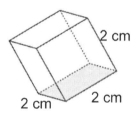

2 cm

2 cm   2 cm

Volume: 8.00 cm³

7)

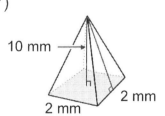

10 mm

2 mm   2 mm

Volume: 13.33 mm³

8)

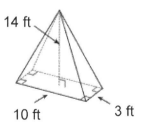

14 ft

10 ft   3 ft

Volume: 140.00 ft³

9)

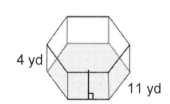

4 yd

11 yd

Volume: 1257.47 yd³

PAGE 70 ANSWERS
ROME WORD SEARCH

Alps   plebeian   patrician   republic
Twelve Tables   Forum   Punic Wars   Pax Romana
gladiators   Colosseum   aqueducts   Christianity
Bible   Rome   Carthage   Julius Caesar
Cleopatra   Augustus   Constantine   Diocletian
Jesus

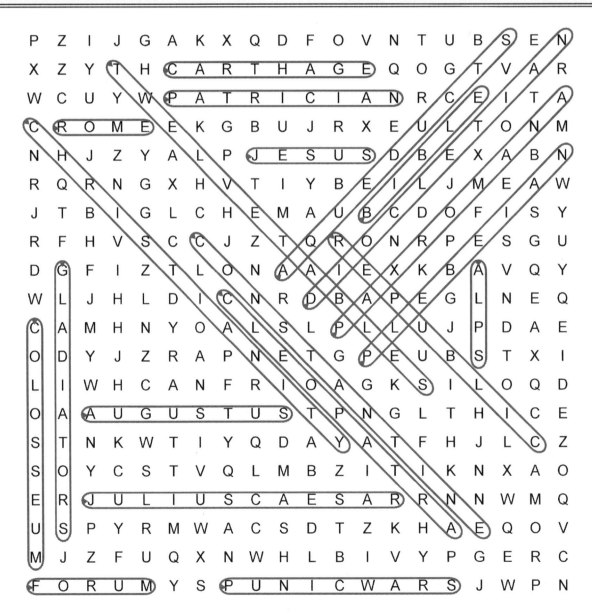

PAGE 71 ANSWERS
SCIENCE DEEP DIVE

Nature of Science

1. What is the difference between an experiment and an investigation?

   Experiment – set of organized procedures
   Investigation – the process of searching for facts or details

2. Provide one example of an experiment.

   Testing medicine to see which is more effective at killing a virus

3. Are steps of the scientific inquiry always the same?

   No – the steps are not always exactly the same

4. What is an example of a scientific observation?

   Example: dogs have four legs and a tail

5. What is an example of analyzing data?

   Example: doing a calculation

6. What is a variable?

   What is changed by the person doing the experiment.

7. What is a procedure?

   An official way of doing something

8. What is a model? Provide one example.

   A replica of the experiment which allows us to visualize difficult concepts

   Example: comet

9. Provide an example of an activity that would be considered scientific?

   Sorting buttons by color and size
   Measuring the height of a plant every day
   Noting how many hours the sun shines each day

10. Define scientific theory. **A well-substantiated explanation which has been tested and corroborated repeatedly in accordance with the scientific method. A scientific theory is accepted as fact until proven wrong.**

11. Provide an example of a scientific law.

    If you drop an object – it will fall to Earth

12. What makes scientific results credible?

    Making sure the experiment has been replicated multiple times to reduce the chance of error

13. Why would a map not be a good model of Earth?

    It is not the same shape of Earth

Our Planet-Earth

14. How does Earth's surface get energy?

    The sun by radiation

15. List the 5 spheres on Earth?

    Biosphere – all living things
    Geosphere – the solid, rocky part of Earth
    Cryosphere – frozen water
    Hydrosphere – liquid water
    Atmosphere – consists of the gases on Earth

16. A glacier is an example of what type of sphere?

    Cryosphere

17. How does water vapor enter the atmosphere?

    Through evaporation

PAGE 73 ANSWERS
SCIENCE DEEP DIVE

18. When the hydrosphere and the atmosphere work together, what are they creating?

    The hydrosphere and atmosphere work together to create the water cycle which creates <u>weather patterns</u>.

19. Which two of Earth's spheres are involved in the water cycle?

    Hydrosphere and atmosphere

20. What would happen if there was no ozone layer present in the atmosphere?

    UV rays would increase and more people would get skin cancer.

21. Which one of Earth's spheres involves water evaporation?

    When water evaporates, it enters the <u>atmosphere</u>

Weathering and Soil

22. Acid rain is an example of what type of weathering?

    Chemical weathering

Erosion and Deposition

23. Which agent of erosion would cause sinkholes?

    Acidic rain

24. Which type of landform is created by glacial erosion?

    U-Shaped valleys

PAGE 74 ANSWERS
SCIENCE DEEP DIVE

Weather

25. What is the difference between weather and climate?

Weather - is the day-to-day state of the atmosphere (or week-to-week) – short term
Climate – the weather of a place averaged over a period of time.

26. What happens to air pressure as you move to a higher elevation?

At higher altitudes the <u>air pressure is lower</u>.

27. What happens when altitude increase?

Air pressure decreases

Climate

28. Which climate factor would affect hurricane movement?

Prevailing winds

29. Which climate has the fastest rate of weathering?

Hot and wet climate

Energy and Energy Transformations

30. What is the difference between kinetic and potential energy?

Kinetic – energy in motion

Potential – stored energy

31. When would a roller coaster have the most potential energy?

At the very top of the hill; before the cart drops down.

32. Provide one example of potential energy transforming into kinetic energy?

    A swinging pendulum each time it changes directions

33. What happens when two like magnets are brought closer to one another?

    They will repel each other

34. If something is about to fall, what is the change in the amounts of energy?

    If boxes fall to the ground, kinetic energy increases and potential energy decreases.

35. Define the term convection. **Heat transfer which occurs through the movement of molecules within fluids (e.g. gases and liquids). Warmer portions rise while colder portions sink. Example: putting a beaker on a hot plate**

Motion and Forces

36. Define the term friction and provide an example.
    A force which resists the sliding/rolling of one solid object against another. Friction always acts in a direction opposite to the direction of motion. Example: using a pencil to write on paper.

37. Define the term unbalanced force. Provide one example.

    Forces acting on an object that cause that object to accelerate.

    Example: two people pulling against each other – one pulling with 50 N and one pulling with 60N

38. Define the term contact force.

    Contact force – push or pull on one object by another object that is touching it.

39. Create a graph that shows the speed of an object staying constant.

    Sample plots (0,0), (2,3) (4, 6) (6,9) (8,12) x – is increasing by 2 / y – is increasing by 3

PAGE 76 ANSWERS
SCIENCE DEEP DIVE

40. Define the term constant speed.

   The object's speed and distance must stay the same (cannot be increasing or decreasing)

41. What is the difference between weight and mass?

   Weight – depends on gravitational force

   Mass – depends on an object's size

   **The more mass = the more gravitational pull

42. What would happen to the weight of a person if gravity disappeared on Earth?

   The weight would become zero.

43. Which type of graph would you use if your data is in the form of percentages?

   A pie graph

Classifying and Exploring Life

44. What are the two parts of a scientific name?

   Genus and species

45. Why would animals be classified under the same genus name?

   If they share similar structural characteristics.

46. Define the term dichotomous key? Why is it important?

   Dichotomous keys are based on structural characteristics. A key for the identification of organisms based on a series of choices between alternative characters.

PAGE 77 ANSWERS
SCIENCE DEEP DIVE

Cell Structure and Function

47. Define the term cell.

The smallest unit of life in any organism

48. What are the 3 principles of the Cell Theory?
    1. **The cell is the smallest unit of life**
    2. **All new cells come from preexisting cells**
    3. **All living things are made of one or more cells.**

49. What are the difference between plant cells and animal cells?

Plant cells have a <u>cell wall</u>, animals cells do not.

50. A large animal is made of how many cells? (Think big)

Trillions of cells

51. Which organelle makes food?

Chloroplast

52. Which organelle is responsible for making proteins?

Ribosomes

53. What is the purpose of a lysosome?

Break down materials

From a Cell to an Organism

54. Write out the levels of organization.

Cell – Tissue – Organ – Organ System - Organism

PAGE 78 ANSWERS
SCIENCE DEEP DIVE

Human Body Systems

55. What is the purpose of the respiratory system?

    To obtain oxygen from the air

56. Which two body systems work together in order to produce adrenaline?

    Endocrine system and nervous system

57. Which two body systems work together to ensure that oxygen gets to all the cells in the body?

    Circulatory system and respiratory system

Bacteria and Viruses

58. What is the #1 way to protect yourself from infectious diseases?

    Wash your hands regularly

59. Why are viruses so dangerous to other organisms?

    They reproduce inside the organisms and cause disease.

60. Can an antibiotic kill a virus? Explain.

    No – antibiotics kill some bacteria, but not viruses

PAGE 79 ANSWERS
EVALUATE 1 VARIABLE

1) -2(5d - 7) use d = 5

    -36

2) 8x - 9 + 4x use x = 8

    87

3) $-\dfrac{15}{c} - 9$ use c = 5

    -12

4) $-\dfrac{s}{8} + 8$ use s = 16

    6

5) $3 + \dfrac{h}{8} - 8h$ use h = 32

    -249

6) k + 9k use k = 4

    40

7) 8k - 7k + 5 - 3 use k = 9

    11

8) 7f - 2(8 - 3f) use f = 8

    88

9) 5(6k - 9) + 2 use k = 5

    107

10) -8c + 9 - 3 + 2c use c = 5

    -24

PAGE 80 ANSWERS
EVALUATE 1 VARIABLE

1) $5x + x$ use $x = 2$

    12

2) $\frac{-8}{z} + 6 + 2z$ use $z = -4$

    0

3) $\frac{c}{2} - 9$ use $c = 8$

    -5

4) $4w + 5w$ use $w = -3$

    -27

5) $2 - 6f - 4$ use $f = -8$

    46

6) $3 + 2k + 8k$ use $k = 6$

    63

7) $2 + 6 + 3w - 8w$ use $w = -8$

    48

8) $-7d + 2(-6d - 9)$ use $d = 3$

    -75

9) $2 - \frac{s}{6}$ use $s = 12$

    0

10) $-8h - 2 + 3 + 5h$ use $h = 9$

    -26

PAGE 81 ANSWERS
MINERAL MATTERS

1. What kind of minerals do we use in materials like fireworks, cement and building stones? *Carbonate minerals*

2. Why would a metal like steel not be a mineral? *It is not a mineral because it is manmade by heating iron with mineral called coke to turn it into steel.*

3. The evaporation of what liquid leaves behind minerals such as halite and gypsum? *Salt water*

4. What two groups are minerals divided into? *Silicates and nonsilicates*

5. What is the range used to measure hardness on the Moh's hardness scale? *1-10*

6. What would be some examples of native elements? *Gold, silver and platinum*

7. Why are your teeth not considered to be a mineral? *Because they are part of and made by your living body.*

8. In the mineral $CaCO_3$, what does the C stand for? *Carbon* What does the Ca stand for? *Calcium* What does the O stand for? *Oxygen*

9. What is a naturally formed, inorganic solid with a definite internal geometric structure called? *It is a mineral*

10. On the Moh's mineral hardness scale, what would be a soft mineral? *Talc*

11. Gold, silver and copper are all examples of what? *Native minerals*

12. What is more reliable than a mineral's color for mineral identification? *The mineral's streak*

13. What is mass divided by volume? *Density*

14. Luster can be described in what three categories? *Metallic, submetallic, and nonmetallic*

15. What special property only applies to a few minerals? *Magnetism*

16. Why would a cake not be considered a mineral? *It does not occur in nature and it does not have a crystalline structure*

17. What can be said of rocks and minerals? *Rocks are made of minerals*

PAGE 82 ANSWERS
MINERAL MATTERS

18. Where would small crystals form due to slow cooling of hot magma beneath the Earth's crust? *Inside the Earth*

19. Why are gold and silver elements? *Because they are only composed of a single type of atom*

20. What is the name given to minerals that contain combinations of carbon and oxygen? *Carbonates*

21. What is the property called of minerals for them to tend to break along flat surfaces? *Cleavage*

22. What color is quartz in its purest form? *Clear*

23. What are the two most abundant elements in the Earth's crust? *Oxygen and silicon*

24. What physical property of minerals can be expressed in numbers? *Hardness*

25. What ore do we get aluminum from? *Bauxite*

26. Are mineral ores renewable or nonrenewable resources? *Nonrenewable*

27. What property of minerals do gem cutters take advantage to cut diamonds and rubies? *Cleavage*

28. What mineral makes up about half the Earth's crust? *Feldspar*

29. When quartz breaks it creates what type of pattern? *A curved pattern called conchoidal fracture*

30. What are minerals called that are composed of only one element? *Native elements*

31. What are gems? *They are minerals that are valued for their beauty rather then usefulness. They are crystalline minerals that are attractive and rare. They are minerals hard enough to be cut and polished*

32. How are minerals most commonly classified? *By chemical composition*

33. What is the color of the powder a mineral leaves behind on a piece of white, unglazed porcelain? *A streak*

PAGE 83 ANSWERS
RENAISSANCE WORD SEARCH

Renaissance	Humanism	95 Theses	Protestants
Reformation	Lorenzo de Medici	Petrarch	Michelangelo
Leonardo da Vinci	Copernicus	Martin Luther	Johannes Gutenberg
William Shakespeare	King Henry VIII	Galileo	

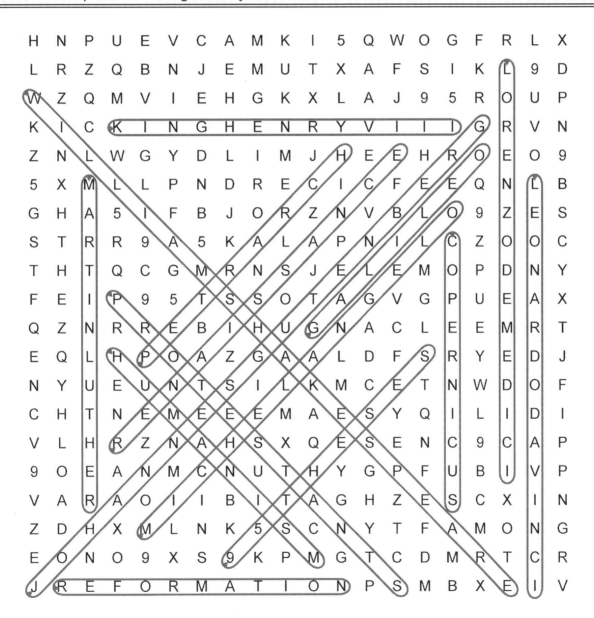

PAGE 84-85 ANSWERS
VERB ROUNDUP

1. has washed
2. has approached
3. has drifted
4. will have solved
5. has played

6. will have recorded
7. has picked
8. had saved
9. will have finished
10. has served

11. A -future perfect
12. B -past perfect
13. B -present perfect
14. A -past perfect
15. C -present perfect

16. C -future perfect
17. C -The dwarves arrived after Snow White had tasted the poisoned apple.
18. A -By the time he finishes, I will have heard that lecture four times this week.
19. A -She has lived there all her life.
20. A -The traffic jam has backed up the cars for two miles.

21. B -It may take all week, but by Friday he will have completed the project.
22. C -present perfect
23. A -present perfect
24. C -past perfect
25. B -past perfect

Made in United States
Troutdale, OR
11/09/2024

24586858R00084